PRAISE FOR DOUG OSTER AND *TOMATOES GARLIC BASIL*

"Doug's writing is equal parts passion and professionalism, conveyed in a comfortable, easy, approachable manner. In this age of vegetable gardening renaissance, this book invites the masses to the party. Bravo!"

– Paul Tukey
HGTV co-host and executive producer
Author of *The Organic Lawn Care Manual*

"For us Southerners, homegrown tomatoes are just about as important as life itself! Doug Oster lays out how to grow them right in this marvelous new book. Garlic and basil as well – with excellent recipes for all three. A must-read for food lovers!"

– Chuck Leavell
Conservationist, author, member of The Rolling Stones
Co-founder of The Mother Nature Network, *www.mnn.com*

"Tomatoes Garlic Basil is a must-have for cooks and gardeners everywhere. Doug Oster clearly has a passion for the three key ingredients of great cuisine. His stories will charm you and his recipes are simple yet elegant (be sure to try the hazelnut pesto)."

– Debra Lee Baldwin
Edibles columnist, San Diego Home/Garden magazine
Author of *Designing with Succulents*

"Part travelogue, part memoir and part cookbook. Doug reveals how he became a gardener to please a beautiful woman – discovering along the way that such women might just be put here to lead men down happy, productive paths. There's just enough gardening info here to get other men into the same kind of wonderful trouble."

– Mike McGrath
Host of NPR's "You Bet Your Garden"
Author of *You Bet Your Tomatoes*

"Doug Oster again lures us to our gardens with humor, engaging stories, and hands-in-the-soil expertise. Beginning gardeners will be guided into their first delicious harvests; experienced gardeners will take it all to a new level. *Tomatoes Garlic Basil* is a delightful guide to three crops that span the gardening year and form the foundation of culinary happiness."

– Nancy Gift
Acting Director, The Rachel Carson Institute
Author of *A Weed by Any Other Name*

"Doug is the next-door garden friend everyone wishes for. His new book weaves together a treasury of hard-earned tips with an engaging personal narrative as he takes on the holy trinity of Italian cuisine."

– Rob Cardillo
Garden photographer, writer

"Tomato-Garlic-Basil: it's the holy trinity of the vegetable garden, and Doug Oster inspires everyone to pick up a trowel. Even more important, he gives a great practical guide to all-natural growing, along with charming stories. We love having him join us on Martha Stewart Living's "Morning Living"!"

– Kim Fernandez and Betsy Karetnick
Hosts of "Morning Living" (Sirius 112 and XM 157)

Tomatoes
GarlicBasil

The Simple Pleasures of Growing and Cooking
Your Garden's Most Versatile Veggies

TOMATOES GARLICBASIL

The Simple Pleasures of Growing and Cooking
Your Garden's Most Versatile Veggies

DOUG OSTER

st. lynn's
press

PITTSBURGH

Tomatoes Garlic Basil
The Simple Pleasures of Growing and Cooking
Your Garden's Most Versatile Veggies

ISBN-13: 978-0-9819615-1-4

Library of Congress Control Number: 2009931952
CIP information available upon request

First Edition, 2010

St. Lynn's Press . POB 18680 . Pittsburgh, PA 15236
412.466.0790 . www.stlynnspress.com

Typesetting–Holly Wensel, Network Printing Services
Cover Design–Jeff Nicoll
Editor–Catherine Dees

Photo Credits
Back cover photo © Matt Freed.
Recipe photos on pages 15, 27, 75, 170, 219 © Doug Oster.
Photo on page 37 © Jessica Walliser.
All other non-recipe photos © Doug Oster.

Printed in China by Global PSD

St Lynn's Press & Global Printing, Sourcing, & Development, in association
with American Forests and the Global ReLeaf programs, will plant two trees
for each tree used in the manufacturing of this book.

10 9 8 7 6 5 4 3 2 1

TO CINDY

You are everything

TABLE OF CONTENTS

FOREWORD

These are extraordinary times in the history of American gardening.

As if on cue, a panoply of developing trends all point towards the garden – opening the gates to the most dramatic resurgence in American gardening since the Great Depression. First and foremost, the economic slump has proven an effective recruiting tool for new gardeners, who reap significant savings by growing their own fruits and vegetables.

This influx of new gardeners has gravitated to the garden for a range of reasons. One contingent started gardening due to well-founded concerns about food safety. Another contingent, the locavore movement, with its emphasis on acquiring locally grown produce, has inspired many who now harvest their food right in their own backyard.

But it is the Baby Boomers who make up the largest portion of these new gardeners. Nearing retirement, their brood of children having flown the nest, they have discovered a creative and rewarding form of recreation. They are the seekers, looking for something they have been unable to find on the Internet, a widescreen TV or their iPhone: authenticity. In the garden they connect to their planet, the seasons and themselves.

The trend towards healthier lifestyles has engendered a veritable gardening army. They've landed in the Great American Garden because they want to fortify their well-tuned bodies with the freshest, most nutritious food they can find. And when the President and First Lady decided to create a vegetable garden on the grounds of the White House, it signaled a welcome national focus on healthy eating.

In his book, *Tomatoes Garlic Basil*, experienced plantsman and seasoned journalist Doug Oster offers the practical advice gardeners need to successfully cultivate these core garden staples in their home garden. Oster's down-to-earth approach to gardening shines through in his writing as he offers easy-to-follow suggestions and advice for common growing questions and concerns most gardeners will come across during their journey in the vegetable patch.

Still, Oster's book is more than a mere gardening guide. His personal insight as a gardener and as a man who is passionate about fresh, healthy foods inspires the reader to think beyond the garden plot for ways to incorporate fresh produce into everyday dishes. It challenges readers to see their vegetable garden as more than just a means to an end, but instead as a vehicle for connecting with children, the community and the soul.

George Ball, Jr.
President, W. Atlee Burpee & Co.

INTRODUCTION

My love affair with tomatoes started as a young boy. I can remember taking a break from climbing the large maple tree in the front of my grandmother's house in Lisbon, Ohio.

From my perch in the old tree, I looked down into the gully between her house and the neighbors and saw her tending her precious tomatoes. I'd never heard of a gully before, but that's what she called it. It was kind of a no man's land, unclaimed territory she decided to make into her garden.

Grandma was wearing a sky blue housecoat lined with a darker blue piping and was pinching suckers off the tomato plants. Up on the hill across the way, the neighbor's white horse looked on, maybe wishing the gully was pasture.

In some ways the memory is crystal clear, the garden scene captured in my head like an old photograph from a Brownie camera. A summer scene in pastels, but this image will never fade; it's been the same for 40 years.

She taught me the right way to water tomatoes, warning me not to get the foliage wet. I listened politely but scoffed, figuring hey, it rains all the time and the foliage gets wet – so I drenched the leaves and let the water run down to the base of the plant. It's funny how smart you think you are at 10.

It wasn't until years later that I learned Grandma was right: Never water the foliage. It's amazing how smart she got as I aged.

That experience with my grandmother led to the creation of my own childhood garden, tended with my mother. The 10-foot-square plot was located in the middle of our one-acre backyard where an above ground pool used to be.

Each summer we put in a few tomatoes. I can still remember the juicy red fruits we picked at the end of the season to enjoy in our salads. I loved those salads. After I'd savored the heart of a head of lettuce with two sliced tomatoes, I'd drink what remained in the bowl – a combination of salad dressing and tomato juice, and it was heavenly.

Now my vice is cold tomatoes with ranch dressing, and when the bowl is emptied I enjoy what's left in the same manner. It's a tradition that takes me back to a simpler time when there were only three TV stations and I ran barefoot all summer around that garden on clover-covered grass, occasionally feeling the sting of honeybees on the undersides of my feet.

Tomatoes link me to my childhood, but garlic was introduced to me by the love of my life, Cindy. Marrying this Italian princess at the tender age of 21 changed the way I would eat and cook for the rest of my life. We have spent countless hours in the garden and kitchen. They are the two most important places to be when things are wonderful in our little world, and when they aren't.

Growing garlic is so rewarding: After a long, hard winter, it can be a religious experience to see the first green shoots poke through the cool spring soil in concert with the crocuses.

It's nirvana to sit in the garden, nibbling on a few of those greens, listening to the birds singing for a mate as westerly breezes bring in the sweet smell of spring. The sun's angle has lifted from its winter low, warming the soil and bathing it in warm orange light at the end of the day.

Garlic is love, and when it hits hot oil in the pan, there's nothing like the smell that fills the house. The aroma drifts out to the garden, making my mouth water like Pavlov's dogs, alerting me to get back to work and finish up so I can run to the kitchen.

Basil is the herb of summer. Just brushing against its leaves releases the sweet fragrance. Embracing this herb was the logical progression after tomatoes and garlic. There's that first day in summer when the perfect storm of gardening hits. The garlic hangs in the tool shed, the basil is deep green reaching for the sky, and then it happens: The first tomatoes are ready for harvest.

Walking into the kitchen with all three in hand brings a hero's welcome from wife and family. Those three simple ingredients fresh from the garden are unbeatable and can create culinary masterpieces only limited by the cook's imagination.

An hour later, sitting around the dining table together as a family and enjoying the garden's most prized treasures – now that's a summer tradition Grandma would be proud of.

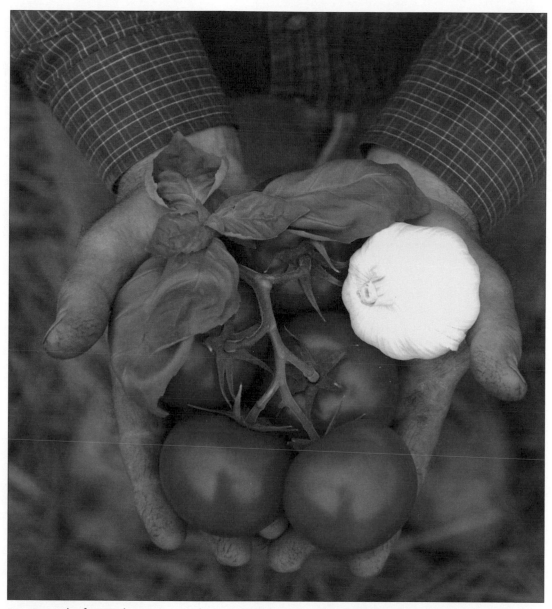

Dan Yarnick of Yarnick's Farm in Indiana, Pennsylvania, with a handful of his tomatoes, garlic and basil.

Part I

FOOD, FAMILY & GARDENS

What was paradise, but a garden full of vegetables and herbs and pleasure? Nothing there but delights.

– William Lawson, 17th C. English horticulturist

1

TEARS IN ITALY

(WHERE I DISCOVER THE CONNECTION BETWEEN HOME-GROWN FOOD AND HAPPINESS)

There is no love sincerer than the love of food.
— GEORGE BERNARD SHAW, *MAN AND SUPERMAN*

It was the trip of a lifetime for my wife Cindy and me. We headed to Italy to celebrate our 25th anniversary – two weeks of heaven. This was only our second trip abroad and I was so nervous that day outside Newark International Airport, I couldn't even finish my beer at a little restaurant in Jersey. That's never happened before…ever.

A couple of hours later, I was sitting in a half-full plane with Cindy and our new Italian friend Gino, having another beer and starting to relax into the feeling of escape from a demanding work schedule and all that goes with raising three children and keeping a roof over our heads.

After we helped Gino smuggle some American cigarettes into Italy he got us a cab outside Rome's Leonardo da Vinci Airport, and that was the last we ever saw of him.

Our first Italian meal was there in Rome, at Trattoria La Toscanella, within walking distance of the Vatican. The antipasto was something to celebrate – simple, fresh and not like anything we were used to back home; the tomatoes, garlic and basil sang to us. Other meals found us sitting on the sidewalks of Rome with a carafe of house wine and plates of simple Italian fare, and really *thinking* about food. What made this kind of food so satisfying? Did it really all come down to something as basic as fresh ingredients? Those two weeks in Italy changed the way we looked at our cooking.

*   *   *

Part of the reason for the trip was to explore the area that Cindy's grandmother grew up in, the Falerna region in the toe of Italy's boot. Her extended family

In Italy Cindy and I got to meet her relatives (l. to r., Giovanni Barletta, his son Roberto, and Cindy). In the background is Castiglione Marittimo, the town where Cindy's grandmother grew up.

from the small village of Castiglione Marittimo greeted us with open arms. We spent three days being wined and dined and touring the sites that Cindy's late Grandmother Righi had enjoyed as a child before she immigrated to the States.

We learned more about how to use tomatoes, garlic and basil from cousin Giovanni Barletta and his wife Mariella, as they served us home-cooked dishes that astounded us – like their transcendent eggplant Parmesan, with its strong taste of basil and a surprising crunchy layer.

Our time spent with the Barlettas was just the beginning of our culinary reorientation. Next stop: Umbria.

*   *   *

They say you can never have a bad meal in Italy and we proved it to ourselves a week later while staying at the farmhouse "Pian della Valle" in the shadow of the hill town Orvieto. Each day we rode our bikes a kilometer and a half to the market to get the day's food for our table. Sometimes the owner wouldn't sell us the produce because of an impending delivery of something even fresher. The fruit and vegetables looked good to us, but they didn't meet his high standards.

When we arrived at the market on a Sunday it was closed. In fact, nearly everything was closed on Sundays, we discovered – just one more thing we took for granted back home, the seven-day buying cycle.

We rode back to our farmhouse wondering what we would do for dinner. We scavenged everything left in the pantry: half a loaf of bread, some dried meats, olive oil, cheeses and some garlic, which our hosts had provided.

We toasted the bread, cooked the garlic and nibbled on everything else. In some ways, sitting there in our rustic kitchen, drinking the local wine and listening to the local radio station playing the latest Italian dance hits, we had to agree: This might be the best meal we've had in Italy. We'd been saying that a lot, lately.

But it was on our last day in Orvieto that the power of food and family finally overwhelmed us. We were at Tipica Trattoria Etrusca, a quaint restaurant tucked into the narrow stone streets of the city. Cindy's first course was a simple red pasta dish. She took one bite and her face took on a look of disbelief. "It's my grandmother's sauce...the exact recipe!" She quickly fed me a bite and I had to agree. We hadn't tasted that perfect mix of spices and pork for more than 20 years, since her grandmother passed away. We thought the recipe had gone with her.

As Cindy savored the next bite, she began to weep and continued crying as she finished every bit of the dish, soaking up the sauce with hard-crusted Italian bread. Everything had caught up to her: experiencing the views her grandmother once enjoyed, walking in her footsteps along the stone streets of Falerna and seeing the ancient cemetery where Giovanni's mother and grandmother were buried.

I tried to explain to the waiter in my bad Italian and using ridiculous hand gestures that there wasn't a problem, that actually this was one of our most wonderful moments in Italy. This woman is crying, I said, because of the emotions your red sauce is evoking.

All it did was confuse him. He never returned to the table, sending another waiter to finish the job. I wanted so badly to explain to the owner how special the moment had been, and to get the recipe for Cindy's grandmother's sauce, but it wasn't meant to be.

Left to right: Tracy Righi (Cindy's grandmother), Cindy Oster holding our son Tim, and Cindy's father Don Righi.

As we stepped back onto the cobblestone streets of Orvieto, the irony was not lost on either of us. We had to come 4,000 miles to get a taste of home.

I wrote a column about it for the *Post-Gazette*. A year later, I got a call from a woman who told me she had taken the story back to the restaurant in Orvieto.

Soon after that, I got an e-mail from another woman, Erica Garcia, who was at that moment visiting in Orvieto and had seen my article posted on the window at Tipica Trattoria Etrusca. Erica asked if they had sent me the recipe yet. When I said no, she got it for me and sent it along.

It's funny how food – something as simple as tomato, garlic and basil turned into sauce – can move so many people.

That's why I wrote this book: to share with you the adventure of growing fresh food and filling your kitchen with irresistible aromas – not to mention, fond memories. I'm betting that after a while, you're going to have your own stories to tell.

And that recipe from Orvieto? It's something we've enjoyed now for years, and every time we eat it, we're reminded of our two weeks in heaven – and of Cindy's beloved grandmother.

Savory Tomato Sauce with Bacon

from Tipica Trattoria Estrusca

The recipe arrived in Pittsburgh in full, authentic Italian form – in other words, it had very little information about specific amounts and cooking times. As the restaurant owner told Erica Garcia (who retrieved the recipe from Orvieto), it is all a matter of taste! You gotta love the Italians. There's a certain magic to doing it this way and I invite you to give it a try yourself.

What You Need:

Olive oil
2 laurel leaves
Basil
Carrots, chopped coarsely
Celery, chopped coarsely

1 16 oz. can of tomatoes, without skin or seeds
1 onion, very finely minced
1 small red pepper ("peperoncino")
Bacon, finely chopped
Salt and pepper, to taste

Here's How:

Sauté the following lightly in olive oil until slightly done: 1 laurel leaf, basil, carrots and celery.

Add tomatoes and cook over low fire for one hour, stirring occasionally.

Remove carrot and celery chunks and purée the rest of the sauce until it's as smooth or chunky as you prefer. If you like a very smooth sauce, pass it through a sieve.

In a medium saucepan, sauté the following in hot olive oil: 1 laurel leaf, onion, and red pepper. When onion is golden brown, add the bacon and cook over low fire until bacon is well done, stirring constantly.

Add the tomato sauce that you've just prepared and simmer over a very, very low fire for about one hour, stirring periodically to make sure it doesn't stick or burn.

Pour over linguini or any other pasta you like, cooked al dente.

Serves 4.

Parmesan of eggs
(Eggplant Parmesan)

When Cindy and I returned from Italy, Cousin Mariella's eggplant Parmesan was still on our minds. How could we have left Italy and not asked for the recipe? By using a computer translation program, we sent an email to the family in Castiglione Marittimo. Here's exactly what we got back. It goes to show you that technology isn't all it's cracked up to be (note that the program simply gives up on a few Italian words completely). But if you study it carefully, maybe you'll get the idea. Here is Mariella's eggplant Parmesan:

Ingredients:

3 grosses eggs, 250 gr of mozzarella, 700 gr tomato of flesh in box or fresh, 2 segments of garlic, 4 leaves of basil, 50 gr of Parmesan grated, 4 olive of oil of spoons, climbs.

You break the eggs and you it it. You it it to slices of about thickness of centimeter means. They cut themselves generally in the length but, if is not very capable with the knife, you it it calmly to washers, it is a little easier one. You systemize the slices of eggs in a large bowl, salting every layer. It is necessary in all a full spoon of salt until: better not to exceed. You put down on the eggs a saucer with a weight, to accelerate the procedure. After a hour about, wrung the slices of eggs between the hands to eliminate more possible water and you it it further between two canvases. It grease just a large pan antiaderente with little oil and you make cook the eggs until will be gilded on two side. You pour a spoon of oil in a pan and make brown the segments of garlic peeled and fragmented, without to make to take color. You unite the flesh of tomato and, after 10 minutes about, when the sauce is not more watery, put out the flame. You unite the basil, salted and passed across a passaverdure. It grease a heat-resistant one and disponetevi a first layer of eggs, sistemandole an of flank to the other one, without them. Does not serve to salt since the eggs detain always a little one of the salt of the salting. You poured 2 spoons of sauce on the eggs and you it it uniform with the back of the spoon. It sprinkle with a little of Parmesan, without to exceed. You cut the mozzarella to thin slice and some distribuitene above the sauce. You it surpassed it between of them. They go well all of the types of mozzarella, but is very comfortable that for pizza, that gives back except for water during the cooking and besides it is cut more easily. It proceed in the same manner until exhaustion of the ingredients. The last layer have to be of sauce, a little more abounding in this case, without cheese. You pour the oil remained on the surface and cook the Parmesan one in the already warm oven to 200° for about 45 minutes.

We did our best with the recipe from what we could decipher. It was good, but it wasn't Mariella's. Feel free to send me any successful variations you come up with.

2

The Joy of Preparing Food You've Grown Yourself

Cooking is like love. It should be entered into with abandon or not at all.
— Harriet van Horne

This book is as much about cooking and enjoying food as it is about growing it. In these pages you'll discover some of my favorite recipes. There's nothing here that's going to worry the great chefs of the world, but then again, they would have a hard time topping the simple elegance of a tomato picked right off the vine, bursting with flavor and ready to eat on the spot...or a few basil leaves on top of a salad.

Though some of the recipes are more complicated than others – and a few even use canned ingredients for the off-season – I hope you will always keep this ethos of freshness and simplicity in mind when spending time in the kitchen. If you're stuck coming up with a menu for dear friends, never forget what might be right outside your kitchen door.

> Simple, fresh and easy – that's what it's about when you're cooking with tomatoes, garlic and basil.

It's really a matter of using the best ingredients available. You can't go wrong with food right out of the garden. And if you stock your kitchen with a really flavorful olive oil, sea salt, fresh-ground pepper and aromatic herbs, you'll be happy you took the extra effort. (Note: In all the recipes that call for olive oil, use the best quality you can find or afford. It makes a difference.)

And don't forget that recipes were once just someone's great idea, so feel free to improvise and play with your food. Cindy and I do it all the time.

Let me share a few examples with you.

A Summer Celebration

While sitting in the garden a few months ago, some ideas came to me for our Memorial Day dinner. These dishes didn't really need a formal recipe to be written down anywhere. You can see how the ingredients just led the way.

I picked four or five of the different tomatoes I was growing, and cut them into slices, which I then laid out on a large platter. In between the tomato slices, I tucked some fresh mozzarella pieces. Then I sprinkled sea salt and drizzled a good, first-press olive oil over everything.

Putting the platter to one side, I tossed a few pinches of salt, several cloves of purple garlic and a bunch of basil onto a cutting board. I chopped it all up as finely as I could and ended up with something like a pesto paste without the nuts. Since olive oil and wine almost always make things better, I added a teaspoon of each to my pile of paste and kept on chopping.

No sooner had I scooped the pesto-sans-nuts into the center of the cheese and tomato platter, it was all gone. We gorged ourselves! The salty pesto was the perfect foil for the creamy cheese and the tangy tomatoes.

Next, it was back out to the garden where Cindy picked fresh lettuce and a few more tomatoes. She mixed it together with a little olive oil and salt. Then I pulled out my secret weapon: balsamic reduction.

This is an easy technique that makes the vinegar sweeter. I just put a quarter cup of balsamic vinegar in a small saucepan and cooked it down under medium heat until it was thick and sticky.

We arranged the lettuce and tomatoes on a small platter with the balsamic reduction dripped into the center of the plate. And we gorged ourselves again, sitting on the patio taking pieces of lettuce and tomato and dragging them through the reduction.

After a long walk in the woods it was time for the main course. Cindy had spent the day making red sauce and also some eggplant Parmesan (attempting yet again to recreate Mariella's magical dish). It was hard to know where we were going to fit in a full entrée after all we had just eaten!

We tried a little of each and knew we'd be enjoying leftovers all week.

I think we're going to forget about burgers and hotdogs on the grill for future Memorial Day celebrations. We've started a new tradition and it will be fun trying to top that meal next year.

What traditions would you like to pick from your garden?

About the Recipes

I've scattered recipes throughout the book, letting them land where they seem happiest. You'll find sauces and condiments, comfort food and classics, side dishes and appetizers, soups and salads, and a few full-out adventures and feasts.

Some thoughts about each of these culinary categories (see the Recipe Finder on page 237):

Sauces & Condiments

These are often the unassuming things you put on top or to the side – and yet they can make a meal. Just taste the difference between a bowl of pasta with red sauce from a jar, versus red sauce from your garden. Or enjoy watching your friends try to put their finger on what that wonderful garlicky flavor is in your chicken sandwich (it's the Garlic Elixir, if you decide to divulge – see page 15). All the recipes in this category concentrate our favorite flavors in some fashion, and often contrast them with surprising new elements (hazelnuts or mango, for example). Let them bring an otherwise simple meal to life.

Comfort Food & Classics

Here are recipes that grandmas have been making for generations. Of course, that doesn't mean that you can't update them or put your own spin on things. You can use any of these as a foundation for something fancier if you like...or not. If you're in a quandary about what to serve your guests, go back to basics. They are everyone's favorites for a good reason.

Side Dishes & Appetizers

These are dishes that shine in small servings, whetting the appetite for the main event. Still, I could happily eat a plate of Basil Fries (page 218) or Fried Green Tomatoes (page 88) for dinner, and just leave it at that, happily. Try to resist the urge to load up your plate, and instead take a moment to arrange just a few bites artistically upon the plate, perhaps with a basil leaf and swirl of balsamic reduction alongside – or even another edible flower or sprig from your garden.

Soups & Salads

I'm not absolutely sure, but it seems that every culture offers some kind of traditional soup and salad. There's something so reassuring and satisfying about them. How often have you come home from an indulgent vacation or a processed-food bender and longed for a fresh, homemade soup and salad for dinner? No need for an entrée here, just mix and match these recipes and you're good.

Adventures & Feasts

These recipes might be considered none-of-the-above. Not because they're weird or taste funny, but because they combine unlikely elements to great effect. I always admire a chef when I sit down for a meal and think, "I never would have thought to do that," and then can't get enough. Maybe good cooking is really all about finding the perfect balance between simple and surprising.

Other than that, all I can say is *buon apetito!* But first, let's get those tomatoes, garlic and basil in the ground!

Garlic Elixir

*My friend Chester Aaron is 86 at the writing of this book. He wanted me to pass along some of the recipes he's used over the years. This one is from his book, **Garlic Kisses and Tasty Hugs** (Zumaya Books). This is kind of an all-purpose garlic condiment that can be used on practically anything from bread, bruschetta, salad dressing, in soup or eaten raw. I invite you to think of more clever uses. It probably explains the "garlic kisses" part of Chester's book title.*

What You Need:

1 cup garlic cloves, peeled
¼ cup parsley
1 teaspoon salt
1 tablespoon red wine vinegar

Olive oil (½ to 1 cup)
1 teaspoon pepper
1 tablespoon lemon juice
Optional: chopped black olives,
red pepper flakes, anchovies or capers, to taste

Here's How:

Process garlic and parsley in a blender until chopped fine, or to your liking. (If you want to add any of the optional ingredients, place them into the blender before you begin blending the garlic and parsley.) Place in a mixing bowl.

Add salt, vinegar, pepper and lemon juice to the bowl, then stir in olive oil until it permeates the mixture, about ½ to 1 cup.

Place in glass jar and cover with ¼ to ½ inch of olive oil to seal. Store in glass jar in refrigerator. Will keep up to a month.

Basil Leaves Stuffed with Cheese and Pine Nuts

Stuffed basil leaves are an easy and tasty starter to a summer meal. Some basil varieties, like 'Lettuce Leaf,' have large leaves that are ideal for stuffing. This recipe combines the flavor of pesto with other interesting textures and tastes.

What You Need:

½ cup pine nuts
4½ oz. soft goat cheese, brought to room temperature. Think about other soft cheeses to use and have fun experimenting. Feta is also a good choice.

3 tablespoons heavy cream
25 large basil leaves
1 large meaty tomato, chopped
4 tablespoons olive oil
Sea salt and freshly ground pepper to taste

Here's How:

In a medium fry pan, toast the pine nuts over low heat, without any oil, until golden brown. About 3 to 4 minutes.

Mix the goat cheese, heavy cream and salt and pepper in a bowl.

Spread about a teaspoon of the cheese mixture on each basil leaf. Then, sprinkle some pine nuts over the top and press them into the cheese. Place the tomatoes on top.

Lightly roll the leaf together, pinching it together near the center. Drizzle with olive oil and serve.

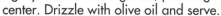

3

Gardens are Good For You

Gardening is about enjoying the smell of things growing
in the soil, getting dirty without feeling guilty, and generally
taking the time to soak up a little peace and serenity.
— Lindley Karstens

You only have to look towards Mediterranean cultures to see the benefits of a diet rich in fresh vegetables.

Scientists have lots of theories about what makes us healthy and not so healthy, but you'd be hard pressed to find anyone who would argue the health benefits of fresh tomatoes, garlic and basil. I won't bore you with research; it just makes sense to me that eating fresh is a good thing.

The act of gardening itself promotes good health, unless you step on a rake, fall off a ladder or cut yourself with a pair of pruners. The wheelbarrow can give quite a workout depending on what's being carried, how far and how often.

But the best thing about gardening really is just being in the garden. Regardless if it's filled with weeds or a manicured pristine landscape, the garden itself is therapeutic. And to me that's the number one health benefit of gardening.

There's an old wooden chair in the corner of my vegetable garden, right next to my tomatoes. I put it there as a place to rest between planting and pushing one of those wheelbarrow loads of compost.

Every season I spend a little more time in that chair, catching my breath between jobs. I like to mix things up as far as garden jobs go. I'll move some compost, do a little weeding, maybe build a little trellis, and then back to the compost. My short attention span gets me to every part of the garden and then back to the comfy chair.

I used to be able to move a few yards of organic matter a day. But now I only want to unload about a yard, and I'm happier when I've got two days to do it in.

One of the things I love to look at are the trees...like the time one late afternoon when the sun hung low in the sky, painting the bark of a pine tree a deep amber, thirty feet in the air. I love just looking as the trees come into leaf and the light changes to illuminate them in different ways. As the season progresses, the songs of the birds change too.

I hung a little birdhouse ten feet from the chair. When I took a break one day, I discovered a pair of Carolina wrens had been building a nest in the gourd-like structure. I sat and watched as they brought nesting materials at a frantic pace. Each day brought new surprises and when I heard the faint chirping of the little babies, I knew I was in for a treat.

The parents ignored me as they hunted for food. My three compost bins nearby provided plenty of insects to feed the little brood. I sat perfectly still, only a few feet from the birdhouse, fascinated. If I stood up or walked towards the nest, both would scream an alarm call.

When the mother or father landed on the edge of the feeder, bug in beak, the tiny birds sang loudly for their supper. There's a moment when the bird lands that it's motionless before it jumps into feed the kids. Each time it has a different insect in its beak, and it's a wonder to watch.

It's not only what you see when sitting quietly in a garden, it's what you hear. It's kind of comforting to hear the neighbors yelling at their kids just like we do. But it's the sound of my old friend the Red-bellied Woodpecker, hidden in the trees, that always brings a smile to my face. I'll hear him calling for a mate starting in late winter and he'll continue into tomato planting season. I think he enjoys my company too; he seems to always be near the garden as I'm working in the soil.

Listening to the birds call to each other is both soothing and intriguing. It doesn't take long to know which bird has which call. The spring air is filled with calls heard only during the mating season. It's the titmice who sound the alarm near the feeder when the cat slowly moves through the tall grass. It usually takes me a while to find her, but the birds know.

One day I heard something behind me and turned to catch a glimpse of movement. Instinctively, I got a shiver up my spine as I heard a snake slither thorough the dry leaves just under the chair. When I saw a tiny two-foot-long garter snake slide through the grass, all I could do was laugh.

But my view of garden life isn't only from that old chair next to the tomatoes. There's a bench along a woodland trail that opened my eyes to the wonders of moss. The tiny seed capsules emerge over the soft green carpet, ensuring another year of life underfoot. I wouldn't have paid it much heed if it weren't for that bench. I might have kept on walking on the trail.

An Adirondack chair hidden in the woods provides a view of the kids who torment me by cutting through the forest. I call it my Fortress of Solitude and I'll sit for an hour at a time up there just waiting for a chipmunk to scurry across the woodland floor, or a little mole to borough through the leaves.

Then there are the kids. Can you imagine being 8 years old, running through the woods and stumbling into a 50-year-old bearded bald guy sitting alone in the forest? "Hello, boys," is all I have to say, and off they go. I guess it's no different than when I used to run through backyards in Warrensville Heights, Ohio, on wash day, plowing into the bright white sheets that hung on close lines.

I've seen and heard many wonderful things while sitting in the garden. It lowers your blood pressure and makes you realize how lucky you are just to be alive and enjoying nature, along with lots of fresh, red tomatoes.

Old-Fashioned Tomato Pie

Tomato pie might sound odd, but this isn't a dessert pie; it's a main course. Sort of like a pizza, surrounded by a flaky crust – and it's amazing.

Savory pies are as common as sandwiches in England, but for some odd reason, we don't eat them much in the US. I served this at one of the cooking/gardening gigs with my radio show partner Jessica Walliser, at Giant Eagle Market District supermarkets around Pittsburgh. When people heard that the recipe was called tomato pie, they looked perplexed, but I got nothing but kudos when I served up the finished prod-

uct. Even the kids were coming back for seconds.

What You Need:

4 tomatoes, peeled and sliced
1 cup chopped basil leaves
1 cup chopped green onions
1 pre-made pie shell or
    make one from scratch

1 cup fresh, imported, grated mozzarella cheese
1 cup grated cheddar cheese
1 cup mayonnaise
Sea salt and fresh ground pepper,
    to taste

Here's How:

Preheat oven to 350° F.

Place the tomatoes in a colander in the sink in one layer. Sprinkle with salt and allow to drain for 10 or 15 minutes.

Layer the tomato slices, basil, and onion in the pie shell. Season the mixture with salt and pepper.

In a separate bowl combine the cheeses with the mayonnaise. Spread mixture on top of the tomatoes and bake for 30 minutes or until lightly browned.

Serve warm. Serves 4 to 6, but I'd bet on 4.

4

KIDS IN THE GARDEN

Forget not that the earth delights to feel your bare feet...
— KAHLIL GIBRAN

There's nothing like having children in the garden. They see things we'll never notice. And it might not even be what's in the garden; they'll look up into the sky and be amazed to see the moon during the day, something we jaded adults take for granted.

My kids are grown now, but we had many wonderful adventures in the garden. Each of mine had their own plots, something I'd forgotten about until I was reading through one of my old garden journals recently.

They grew tomatoes, beans, marigolds, peas and anything else they were interested in. I came across an old video of my two boys telling me what they wanted to grow in their gardens. The list was hilarious, as it included more than a large truck farm could grow. Later, my young daughter would sit in the garden picking dandelion flowers and looking for worms (sometimes to eat).

Whenever their friends would visit I'd find ways to get them to try some of my heirloom tomatoes or some other unusual thing. I know it's a leap of faith for anyone to try a ripe 'Green Zebra' tomato for the first time, so to watch a kid get up the courage to bite into that yellowish green striped tomato...well, that's pretty near priceless. It's one of those moments when they realize something doesn't have to look a certain way to taste great.

Those days have passed, but our neighbors have two wonderful little children who will come up to the garden with their father, and I have the pleasure of introducing them to garlic greens, dandelion leaves, white tomatoes and herbs, like mint and basil. They're brave, too. I've told them there's just one rule of the garden when it comes to trying new things: "If you don't like it, spit it out – you're not at dinner with the Queen of England."

During the summer when I see them playing in the woods I call them over, give them some produce and maybe a cut flower for their mom. They even bring their friends to try the strange wonders I grow. It's great to have young faces in my garden again, even if it's just once in a while.

Our boys Matt (l) and Tim in our first garden in Stow, Ohio.

My kids were the reason I went organic. I was using chemical pesticides and didn't understand how dangerous they might be for the family, until the day I had my epiphany. I'd just applied Sevin to some cabbage plants when my youngest son, Matt, a toddler, walked down the garden path barefoot in search of fresh snow peas – about to walk through the poison powder. I grabbed him up in a hurry. It was the last day I ever used chemicals in the garden and I've never looked back.

I used to love to see my kids out in the garden as the sun was setting behind them. In springtime they'd feast on those snow peas and garlic greens, then tomatoes later in the season. After my epiphany I knew each bite they took would not only be tasty, but safe too.

In the garden now, my kids have gotten too old for the wonderment of years past. They just ask when the tomatoes will be ready to eat and have to be dragged outside to take a look, something they do reluctantly to placate their old dad. Maybe we'll reminisce about what we grew and ate together, and how it was a happy summer gathering place for our family.

Now, it's a quiet place for my wife and me to come and just sit. It's still a happy place to be. Time changes everything, and luckily the garden evolves with us and we evolve with it.

5

Gardening in the City

"Where you have a plot of land, however small, plant a garden.
Staying close to the soil is good for the soul.
— Spencer W. Kimball

On a recent trip to New York City for my 50th birthday I was struck by how many urbanites actually were growing gardens on balconies, rooftops and front stoops.

I live on four acres, just seven miles from downtown Pittsburgh, but I've seen great gardens grown among tall buildings and row houses. All you need is the same inspiration that drives us all to grow our own produce.

In the city, gardeners can take advantage of the heat retained in the concrete jungle. It's often much warmer downtown than out in the 'burbs. In the spring and fall that's a great thing; in the summer it could be a problem.

❧ CONTAINER GARDENING ❧

Traditionally, an urban garden relies on pots and the familiar planter boxes. But today, there's something called an Earth Box, a patented, self-contained growing system, and it may be one of the greatest inventions of the 21st century for container gardeners. It's great for growing just about anything and perfect for creating a garden in the city (the Earth Box folks didn't pay me to say this, but when I see something that works I like to share the news).

The box is about 30 inches long, 14 wide and 12 deep. It comes with everything you need for a great harvest, including a potting mix and fertilizer.

One of the best features an Earth Box has to offer is the water reservoir. If you don't get to watering every day in the heat of the season, you'll be all right. The box is also covered with plastic to stop weeds and keep the soil inside both moist and warm.

I'd only plant one tomato in each, but I've seen them growing two. You could get away with three peppers and countless leafy lettuce plants; the possibilities are endless.

The lesson learned from the Earth Box is to use containers that are big and filled with a nutrient-rich medium that will give your plants everything they need.

> Using the biggest containers possible and mulching them will allow for a more relaxed watering schedule, and less work for you.

WHAT GROWS WELL IN POTS

When deciding what to grow, take into account how much sun the area gets. Most vegetables are sun lovers and that includes tomatoes, basil and garlic.

Tomatoes

Certain varieties of tomatoes lend themselves well to containers because of their smaller growth habits, but that doesn't mean you can't grow an eight-foot-tall plant in a pot. It just needs the right-sized pot and good support for the vines. (For a more complete discussion of container tomato planting, see Chapter 17).

Basil

There's just nothing like big leafy basil plants in summer, and they will thrive in containers. Every year I fill a large pot with a couple of plants right outside the kitchen door for easy access. But if your space is really limited, the smaller 'Spicy

Globe' basil might be a better choice than the common leafy type. It's got the basil taste only with a little kick. The plant stays compact and bushy, making it a natural for growing in pots.

Garlic? Maybe Not

Garlic is a tough one to grow in containers, since in most cases the cloves will overwinter in the pot. The soil must stay moist, but can't be soaking wet or the bulbs will rot. I always recommend planting garlic in the soil.

But if that's not an option, try this: Plant the garlic as described in the garlic chapter, only use a container filled with a good planting mix that's moist. The pot needs to get cold during the winter, but keep it in a spot that won't get rain or snow. In the spring, bring the container out in the open and let the early season rains do their job. The garlic greens will sprout, offering delights that only gardeners get to sample.

FINDING SPACE FOR A GARDEN

In the city, even a small strip of land can be used for growing tomatoes, garlic and basil. So, if your deck or patio isn't enough for your gardening urges, consider expanding your horizons.

Vacant Land

Is there an unused bit of land next to your building? Be aware that the soil could have some chemical history, and test for heavy metals first; if they're found, it's going to be a challenge to remove them before planting. I'm not sure about the science of nasty stuff like lead in the soil, but I don't want to eat tomatoes grown there.

If you're confident that your place in the sun is lead-free, then treat it just like any garden and put down lots of organic matter before you plant.

Even if the soil is not welcoming, here's a way around that: I have friends who built up raised beds 18 inches deep over rough concrete and bricks. They add compost to the beds each year and grow a great city garden.

There's no reason that city dwellers can't grow their own vegetables, it's just a matter of being creative in finding the right spot to grow them.

A Community Garden

Another option is finding a community garden plot. In New York City, I was surprised to see them tucked between row houses. I'm guessing that some gardens can be found right around the corner from where you live, while others might be large plots of land a little way outside of town.

Community gardens offer a plot to people who don't have room to grow what they want at home. The plots are often coveted, often require advance registration and sometimes a fee to cover the costs of water, fencing, compost and more.

What's great about community gardens is the camaraderie that's established between like-minded people. Gardening can be thought of as a solitary practice, but community gardens change that in a good way. There's always someone there who can help with questions, or to watch over your piece of the garden.

One downside is that, come harvest time, it can be hard to stop others from harvesting your hard-earned work. This always depends on the location of the garden. Most are posted asking visitors to look but don't touch. One I visited in New York had a sign on the gate requiring visitors to be accompanied by a gardener growing something inside.

Some of the best gardeners I've ever met spent their summers in community gardens. Maybe you'll meet them there, happily offering tips to help others harvest the best produce possible. Maybe one of these days you'll be the one offering tips to the newly minted gardeners in the community patch.

There's no need to think you have to have four acres in the country to garden, when the urban landscape is so full of fertile opportunities too.

Basil Mimosas

How about kicking off your day with this twist on the traditional mimosa? This is a wonderful summer drink that can be served on the patio or for a tour of the garden. It's easy to make, but it takes two days, so start the night before.

What You Need:

12 oz. orange juice (fresh squeezed is best, of course!)
1 to 1½ cups whole basil leaves
3 cups water
½ cup lemon juice
½ cup sugar
1 bottle Champagne (or any nice sparkling wine)

Here's How:

Combine orange juice, water and basil in a pitcher. Let steep 4 hours, then strain out the basil.

Add the lemon juice and sugar and stir until the sugar is dissolved.

Refrigerate overnight.

To prepare a mimosa, fill a glass half full with the flavored orange juice. Add a spike of basil flowers, then fill the remainder of the glass with champagne and enjoy!

Part II

SOME GARDEN BASICS

When I go into the garden with a spade, and dig a bed, I feel such an exhilaration and health that I discover that I have been defrauding myself all this time in letting others do for me what I should have done with my own hands.

– Ralph Waldo Emerson

6

A Word About Soil

To forget how to dig the earth and to tend the soil is to forget ourselves.
— Mahatma Gandhi

Gardeners have sayings, and they like repeating them; I know I do. The stories morph as each gardener embraces them and passes them along. This chapter's saying goes something like this: "Dig a $40 hole for a $20 tree."

That says it all when it comes to preparing the garden for planting. If you want your garden to flourish, you'll need to get the soil in shape by adding organic amendments. I mentioned that in the Introduction, but here are some more tips for getting nutrient-rich soil that will help your plants (and everything else your garden) thrive.

Plan Ahead

Experienced growers actually get their tomato beds prepared the year before (I was out in my garden on a recent Christmas Eve, adding horse manure).

Cover Crops

Along about fall, when the last of your tomato vines have been wrestled into the compost pile, you can start thinking about prepping your soil for the spring growing season. I'm talking about laying down a cover crop.

Winter rye is easy to find and my favorite. If you spread the seeds on the ground in late September they will usually sprout before winter arrives. The rye (or whatever grass or legume you use) holds the precious soil in place so that the wind can't erode it, and the mineral nutrients won't be leached away in the winter rains. Cover crops have other benefits too, such as providing habitat for beneficial insects.

In spring, you can cut the crop and turn it back into the soil. Now you've got green manure.

✄ SOME SOIL ENRICHING TRICKS ✄

Once it's springtime and you think you've got the soil right where you want it, you'll want to know about a couple of tricks that have been passed down for generations.

Epsom Salts

Gardening folklore says to add a couple of teaspoons of Epsom salts to the planting hole. Though I've never done this, the theory is that the Epsom salts (magnesium sulfate) add magnesium to the soil and give it a boost. I haven't seen the science behind this, but I know a lot of gardeners that swear by it, so that's good enough for me. Maybe one day I'll give it a try with a few plants – put some into the planting holes and see how those plants compare to those without Epsom salts.

Eggshells

The second trick, which I use myself – and which has little or no basis in science – is to add crushed eggshells when you plant tomatoes. I've done it for years, at the suggestion of an old gardening friend. Eggshells purportedly add calcium to the soil, which will help fend off blossom end rot (that's a condition caused by a lack of calcium, resulting in a dark sunken spot on the underside of the tomato). How long does it take those eggshells to release their calcium and start to work?

Your guess is as good as mine; all I know is that my plants don't suffer from blossom end rot.

A TIP ABOUT BLOSSOM END ROT

Certain varieties, oftentimes paste tomatoes, can be prone to the disease. Even if you toss a dozen eggshells into a planting hole, that alone won't make you 100% safe from blossom end rot. The problem may not be about lack of calcium, but lack of water. There may be adequate calcium present in the soil, but the plant can't get it if the soil is too dry. So keep mulching your tomatoes and giving them water when the soil is dry.

Soil Test Kits

I've never used one, because I feel that adding organic matter every year is providing the things the plants need, and everything grows well for me when I do that. But if you have questions about pH or soil fertility, then it's a good idea to get a soil test. Local state extension offices offer test kits that are cheap and easy to use. See the resources list at the back of the book for more information.

Most of all, listen to your fellow gardeners. If you admire their garden, then take their advice – they are probably doing something right.

7

COMPOST

I am open to the accusation that I see compost as an end it itself. But we do
grow some real red damn tomatoes such as you can't get in the stores...
Makes you wonder.
— ROY BLOUNT, JR., AUTHOR, HUMORIST

I've always believed that any gardener worth their salt has a compost pile. The
first one I ever saw was at my neighbor's house. Mrs. Kelly had a huge pile of
rich, black compost, and it was obvious that stuff worked, because she had the
best garden in the neighborhood.

What's so great about compost? Good compost has everything your plants will
need to keep them happy for the entire season. Even if my soil is amended with
manures and other good stuff, I always put some of my wonderful homemade
compost into the planting holes. If there's any compost left after planting, I use it
as mulch around the plants, then every time it rains, nutrients from the compost
leach down to the roots of the tomatoes. I find there's never enough compost for
everything in the garden, so I (and maybe you) will have to choose what plants
deserve the best stuff, and when.

You can go to your garden center and buy composted soil in bags, but why
spend the money when you can make the same stuff, or better, right at home –
and have the pleasure of doing it yourself? If you live in an apartment or your
home has no garden area for a compost pile, then the store-bought bags will do

fine for your container-grown tomatoes or other plants. But if you've got even a modest yard out back, you've got the perfect setup for making some first-class compost.

It Starts In the Kitchen

Making compost is easy because anything that was once living will turn into the soft, black, nutrient-rich material. The key to setting up a composting system indoors is splitting the stream between what goes to the pile and what is sent to the curb. It's always surprising to first-timers how much of what's produced in the kitchen can be recycled. It won't take long to get everyone in the house into the habit of putting compostable food scraps directly into a kitchen composting pail. And from there, out it goes to your compost pile.

All of us want to be able to harvest our beautiful black compost as soon as possible, and some types of piles work faster than others. My system is simple, and good for someone who's too lazy or too busy to fool around with the standard method of turning...and turning...the pile. I do it with three small compost bins.

How I Make Compost

My three compost bins are right outside the vegetable garden. The bins are made out of wood pallets, making up the four sides of a roughly a three-cubic-foot block of material. (One of these days I'm hoping to find something a little bigger to form the bins.)

It's a 1,2,3 process that almost takes care of itself. The bins sit next to each other in the woods at the edge of my garden. Full disclosure: They will need to be replaced about every ten years, as the wood starts to rot.

Step 1: I fill the first bin with garden refuse, kitchen scraps, coffee grounds, vegetable and fruit trimmings, unbleached paper towels, eggshells...you name it.

The only things I don't put in are meats, oils and dairy products – not because they won't compost, but because they can attract rodents. I know people who include meats and the other things you're not supposed to add, and never have a problem. I just don't want to chance it.

Steps 2 and 3: Once that first bin is filled, I start filling the second, then the third.

Voila! At some point, usually by the time number 2 is filled, number 1 is ready to harvest. It's that easy.

What just happened in those bins? During the decomposition process the compost pile heats up. When built right, it will reach 160°F. Dig into that pile while it's cooking and you'll see what I mean.

A 3-bin compost system, hard at work.

How Much of What Goes In?

There are specific ratios of certain materials in order to make perfect compost – I don't bother trying to be too exact. What I produce works fine for me.

There are two basic types of material that you add to the compost pile: **green** and **brown**. The greens are things coming fresh out of the garden and kitchen. The browns are fall leaves, paper products, dried grasses…things like that.

The perfect ratio (depending on who you ask) is 50/50 by volume. Every time you add a 5-gallon bucket of greens, add the same size bucket of browns. When I add the greens I often add some leaves that I keep piled next to the bins. In my case, it helps prevent animals from foraging around inside (the leaves aren't all that tasty).

Turning Is Optional, and Gets You There Faster

If you want finished compost quicker, all you have to do is keep the pile moving, instead of just letting it sit there. Turning it over (a digging fork works best) will accelerate the decomposition process. Garden writer and radio host Mike McGrath says that anyone who says they turn their compost pile is a liar. I'm not sure I'd go that far, but turning the pile can be a chore.

Love That Smell!

Once I get a bin filled, I like to leave a little depression on top so that the pile can collect rainfall. If the pile begins to smell like old rinds, it means it needs more air; get in there with a fork and open it up a bit, and the smell will be gone in a day or two.

When the compost is done, it's black, fine and sweet-smelling. Because there's always something that doesn't get broken down, like corn cobs, I use a sieve made of hardware cloth and 2 x 4's to sift the compost. Anything the sieve catches (that can be composted) gets thrown over into the next bin. You'll also find other things that made their way into the pile, like forks *(Oh, that's where they went!).*

Mrs. Kelly would be proud of me now if she saw the compost I made in the woods adjoining my vegetable garden. I'm glad to be recycling all the things that should never go to a landfill. And at the end of the season when my tomatoes are happy and healthy I can point to the compost pile, just as she did, as the reason they thrive.

German–Italian Risotto with Basil, Tomatoes and Corn

Risotto is Italian comfort food, somewhere between rice and pasta. It's not tricky to cook, but has to be done just right to get the perfect firm-but-creamy texture. If you happen to grow your own corn this is a great way to use a few ripe ears – as long as you can get to it before the raccoons do.

This recipe is inspired by a trip to Germany where, I discovered, they serve pasta with corn. I love the sweetness of the corn mixed with all the other savory flavors.

What You Need:

For the tomato, basil and corn mix:
4 ears of corn
1 large meaty garden tomato, chopped
2 cloves garlic, minced
½ cup of fresh basil, chopped
4 teaspoons olive oil

For the risotto:
3½ to 4 cups chicken broth
4 tablespoons butter
5 to 10 green onions, finely chopped
1 cup arborio rice
Sea salt and freshly ground pepper to taste
½ cup dry white wine
½ cup freshly grated Parmigiano Reggiano cheese
2 tablespoons butter

Here's How:

Take 4 ears of corn and cook them the way you usually do. That might mean in boiling water for a few minutes. However, I was once told by a reliable source that that's how you ruin corn. As I understand it, corn should be roasted, which I love. It's filled with a wonderful flavor. I soak the ears in water for 1 minute, then throw them on the grill for about a half hour, in a spot where they get indirect heat.

As soon as the corn is done, throw it in ice water and then remove the kernels with a sharp knife.

For the tomato and basil mix: Combine the corn, tomato, olive oil, basil and garlic. Add sea salt and pepper, to taste

In a medium saucepan bring the chicken broth to a slow, steady simmer.

At the same time, in another medium saucepan, heat the butter and then add the green onions. Cook for a few minutes until translucent.

Add the rice and stir for a couple minutes, making sure all the grains are well coated with butter.

Add the wine and stir until the rice absorbs the wine. Then add the hot chicken broth while stirring slowly – just pour a little in. Let the rice absorb it, and then pour more in.

After about 15 to 20 minutes (stirring occasionally throughout), add a little more broth if needed. Just like pasta, it's done when it's tender, but firm. You'll get the feel for it.

Remove from heat, add the corn and cheese, and season to taste.

Add the tomato basil mix and serve warm.

Serves 4 to 6.

8

Curbside Treasures

One man's junk is another man's treasure.
— Author unknown

There's often a frugal nature to gardeners, and I love it. Frugality is especially strong if they lived through the Great Depression.

My parents were born at the start of the Depression and instilled in me a sense of what money is worth, and that's why I'm a trash picker and proud of it.

Getting something at a bargain – or better yet, for free – makes me smile.

My kids hate it when we're driving along in the truck and I see something of interest at the curb to add to the garden. I have no qualms about pulling over and loading the treasure(s) into the bed.

I've rescued pots, flats, benches, statues, tables, furniture, tools, plant stands and more. My latest find was a mint condition compost tumbler.

I've always wanted one, but I'm too cheap to drop nearly $500 for a good one. I first spotted it on the side of the road, set back behind a brick mailbox holder in front of a business. I wasn't sure if they were setting it out for the trash or just putting it there for someone to pick up. It didn't matter, because that particular day I was in a hurry and couldn't stop. I figured I'd never get it. That's how it works in the world of curbside wonders – drive by and forget it; some other cheap bastard will descend on the item after you pass by.

A couple of days later I was trying to remember where I saw it, and as I drove down the road about a mile from my house, I saw it again.

I couldn't believe my luck. It was around 11 in the morning, and I went into the karate studio behind where the tumbler was sitting. No one was in the front part of the building but a curt voice from upstairs yelled, "Who is it?" I looked up and saw a scary looking karate guy looking back down at me. "Are you giving away that green thing out there?" I asked. He explained that it belonged to the business next door.

I thanked him and hopped back into the truck to make the short trip around that mailbox to the next business. As I pulled around the property line divided by privet shrubs, I realized it was a massage parlor.

Now, I've got nothing against massage parlors or guys that go in them; it's just not my thing. As an aside, I had just gotten off a TV appearance and I was wearing the same khaki shirt I always wear. It kind of brands me and it helps people recognize me more readily. Which is usually a good thing.

But here I was that morning, on a busy street close to home. I knew what would happen if I went in there: As soon as I came out, either a group of garden-loving priests would drive by or a carload of my wife's dearest friends. A lose-lose situation.

I looked over my shoulder at the tumbler and saw what pristine condition it was in and I was inspired. *"I'm going in,"* I said to myself.

Inside, I was greeted by an Asian woman who had a sweet smile but couldn't understand what I was trying to convey to her as I mimed cranking a composter. I motioned her to come with me to the door so I could show her. She put on a pair of sandals, and as I stood at the front door pointing out at the composter and making my plea, a woman I knew drove by.

I swear she looked at me with a furrowed brow and disappointed look on her face, but I can't be sure. Maybe she didn't know it was me. I'm not going to mention it next time I see her.

Anyway, I got the tumbler, loaded it into the truck and drove it home.

My wife got quite a laugh out of my predicament, but was thrilled to have somewhere to put fresh compost that would not require a quarter-mile walk out to the compost piles.

Another addition to the garden that didn't cost a dime. It took me a week to wipe the smile off my face. Now that's a happy ending.

9

WEEDS

"Many things grow in the garden that were never sown there."
— THOMAS FULLER, *GNOMOLOGIA*, 1732

There's one thing in the garden that never needs help growing, and that's weeds.

I'm not the type of gardener that uses sprays to deal with them and certainly I'd never put anything in the garden that wasn't organic. Even organic herbicides don't appeal to me.

There is an irony in the fact that I think it's OK to bring my Stihl trimmer into the garden; it's certainly not organic and the emissions don't help the environment, but it's easy and effective, so maybe I'm no different than anyone else in that I pick my poison.

There's no single best way to keep weeds at bay for every situation, so I'll give you a number of good ones to choose from.

Topcutting

One surefire way to control tough perennial weeds is continued top cutting of the foliage. By removing that above-ground growth, you deprive the roots below of the energy provided by the greens. The trick is to keep after them; a weekly decapitation for even the toughest weeds will be an effective deterrent against them.

Whether it's poison ivy or even Japanese knotweed, top killing works. A word of warning about poison ivy and poison oak: If you're highly allergic, leave this job to someone else.

Hoeing

A sharp hoe is a great tool for weeds, too. The key work is sharp. Of all the different types of hoes out there, I like the old-fashioned kind, and in fact I use my grandfather's old hoe. There are lots of ways to sharpen it. A real man would use a file or a grinder, but I use something called Accusharp. I bought it years ago and it's a hand held tool that runs along the business end of the hoe, shovel, pruners or whatever needs to be sharpened.

Pulling

Pulling weeds is the last resort. It's painstaking and hard, but some people find it therapeutic. Whatever floats your boat, right?

Torch 'Em

Another way to control weeds without chemicals is to burn them out. This is most effective when dealing with weeds that aren't around your precious plants. The torch is propane powered, great for in-between flagstone or on paths between vegetable beds.

A word to the wise: You've got to be careful when working with an open flame. Always have a hose ready. Once, I was burning up an old picnic table in a large grill, piece by piece, when one of the pieces fell out of the grill and started the nearby dry grass on fire. I ran to the garden hose and turned it on, but all I got was a trickle; the hose was kinked somewhere along its 150-foot length. Luckily, it was enough water to stop the flames and I avoided setting the forest on fire – but barely.

Common Dayflower. Lots of gardeners call this small annual an annoying weed. But I think the flower is so pretty I let it grow in my garden undisturbed.

Smothering

In my vegetable garden I use a weed abatement and prevention technique often credited to the late Ruth Stout; she was an organic pioneer who used layers of organic matter to plant in. Following her lead, I just cover the weeds with mulch, specifically straw. It has another benefit too; not only does it smother the weeds, it keeps the soil evenly moist – a bonus for tomatoes, garlic and basil. Ruth Stout has inspired me, along with the co-authors of *Teaming with Microbes*, Jeff Lowenfels and Wayne Lewis, to try no-till gardening and it has changed the way I look at weeds and how I deal with them.

No-Till Gardening

In no-till gardening, the soil is not disturbed, it's just built up by adding organic matter every year – the theory being that there's a symbiotic relationship between all sorts of organisms underground, and every time we dig up the soil that relationship is destroyed.

I've had a couple of seasons under my belt and couldn't be happier. Every fall I cover my beds with well-aged animal manures and compost. Sometimes I'll add a cover crop of winter rye. To beat the weeds in the manure, make sure it's completely composted. A good compost pile reaches 160°F in the center and kills not only seeds, but many pathogens, too.

Newspapers

As soon as the winter rye gets cut down each spring, we turn our attention to the weed control. Since the soil is ready to go, I can now lay newspapers on the beds to stop the weeds. Trust me, this method works! Newspapers are safe to use, since they are printed with soy and water based inks. Any newsprint is fair game, just don't use the shiny color inserts.

Lay them on, about 10 pages thick, spray them down with water to hold them in place and then cover them with mulch. Now you can just push a little mulch to the side and gently poke a hole in the paper to set in your transplants.

You won't have any weed problems and the newspaper will just decompose. At the end of the season, start the cycle again by adding the organic matter.

Cardboard

Often a hard item to recycle, cardboard makes a great weed preventer that will eventually just rot away.

Black Landscape Fabric

This is a great way to cover beds after they've been prepared. It lets water and air through, but not light, so weeds can't sprout. Another benefit is that it warms the soil – perfect for tomatoes, garlic and basil. After the garden beds are ready, lay the fabric down and hold it in place with rocks, soil or galvanized pins (available at most garden centers). Now, just cut a hole for the plants and put them into their summer home.

Corn Gluten Meal

If the bed is going to be planted with seeds, wait until the weeds sprout, then put down some corn gluten meal. It's conventionally used for lawn treatment to stop annual weeds from sprouting. The corn gluten dries out the seed right after germination, stopping it from growing.

Sometimes corn gluten will be mixed with an organic fertilizer for lawn treatments so you get weed control and a boost for the plants. The corn gluten itself adds some nitrogen to help things grow.

A Living Mulch

This is related to the smothering concept, above, but much more decorative, and also a great way to stop weeds in the garden. Consider planting something low-growing, like thyme in your beds. You can interplant your food crop as you go.

Crowd 'Em Out

One way I beat the weeds is to crowd them out with other plants. By planting close together, the weeds are shaded out (they need sunlight to thrive).

For garlic: I plant the bulbs about six inches apart in October and then mulch them with a thick layer of straw. Next spring when they sprout, I apply another layer of straw. This is also a great time to apply corn gluten meal. As the plants grow, they cast shade on the ground below. Some weeds will sprout, but are easily hand pulled; they can't get a good hold. Between struggling to push through the straw and reaching for the light under the green leaves of garlic, it's all just too much for them.

For basil: I plant these close together, around eight inches apart. They quickly touch each other, forming an impenetrable canopy to the weeds below.

The Philosophy of Weeds

There's also a time and a place to let the weeds go...yes, give them their freedom. Remember, a weed is just a plant growing in the place we don't want it to. A corner of the garden left wild will help attract a wide variety of beneficial insects. It's also a good idea to have as many different plants in the garden as possible and if there are some weeds that are beautiful, why not?

But what is beauty? Only you can answer that question. For years I've been battling the 'Common Dayflower,' even though people visiting my garden will ask about the plant, thinking I chose to put it there. The only reason I used to pull it was that I called it a weed.

This season I let them go and enjoyed the stunning, luminescent, small sky-blue flowers in mid-summer.

A Time to Eat...Dandelions

Today in my garden, I don't consider dandelions weeds; they are a tasty plant with a beautiful flower. I love the leaves in salads and they are one of the most nutritious plants on the planet. That's why it's such an irony that it's so reviled.

Growing on the outside of my raised basil and garlic beds are dandelion plants, enjoying the good soil. They thrive in compost-rich earth, the leaves are less bitter and the foliage remains tender.

When harvesting dandelion leaves, be sure they were never treated with herbicide. Knowing where they come from is the most important aspect of enjoying them from the garden. That's why I only pick my own.

The absolute best time to pick them is in early spring, before the little flower bud emerges in the center of the crown. Once that happens the leaves become more bitter.

After the flowering cycle is over, you can begin harvesting again. Just cut the entire plant down to the ground and wait; the leaves that re-emerge taste almost as good as the early spring crops.

Once, while I was doing a cooking demonstration on KDKA-TV, making my Salmon in Dandelion Sauce, I mentioned that dandelion was an acquired taste. Anchor Brenda Waters put a raw leaf in her mouth and laughed, saying, "I ain't acquired it yet!"

The crew gobbled up the finished recipe, though, and even Brenda admitted it wasn't so bad. She asked for some more to be left on the side to eat later.

COOKING TIP: *Dandelions also pair perfectly with tomato sauce and can be mixed with balsamic vinegar to balance the bitterness of the greens.*

Whether you embrace, eat or hate your weeds, just be assured that there are plenty of ways to get rid of them without the use of harmful chemicals. Whatever else you choose to do is between you and your weeds.

10

FOUR-LEGGED PESTS

Lots of people talk to animals... Not very many listen, though... That's the problem.
— BENJAMIN HOFF, *THE TAO OF POOH*

Sharing your produce with friends and family is one thing, but losing it to four-legged marauders is another.

My friend Mary Robb Jackson, a reporter from KDKA Television in Pittsburgh, couldn't keep the deer out of her suburban garden. She knew something was destroying her tomatoes, and those telltale hoof prints gave away the invaders. It was the end of the season and she hadn't been able to harvest much because of her unwanted visitors.

One day, Mary Robb was in the garden at dusk one day, when she saw a deer standing in the woods just outside her garden. Frustrated and overcome with anger, she threw the closest thing she could get her hands on at the animal, a ripe tomato.

Fencing: How High...What Kind?

The best way to keep animals out of the garden is to put up some kind of fence. The type and height of fence depends on which pest is after your tomatoes and basil.

Garlic is relatively safe, though. It will rarely be bothered by something that wants to eat it, but animals on their way through the garden to get to your other

51

Some of the raised beds in my home garden. Note the perimeter fence with the 7' fence posts. That's in case the deer start jumping in and I need to put in higher fencing.

plants could trample the tender greens. Deer are browsers and are the most likely culprit to crush the garlic while headed towards the tomatoes (unless there's a rabbit stampede).

Plastic Netting

Keeping deer out of the good-sized garden requires a fence that's seven feet tall, and even though they could leap it in a pinch, they would prefer to run around it.

The cheapest way to fence the garden at that height is to use thick plastic netting. I use it tacked up on trees and posts and it's very effective in stopping deer browse.

I've got lots of deer pressure – a herd that's doubled in ten years to 22. Yes, they're beautiful, but only outside the garden. My vegetable garden is relatively small, about 30' x 40'. When your enclosed space is small like that, deer think it's a trap and are less likely to try to jump inside. They don't normally jump into enclosed spaces. That's the theory, anyway, and so far, it's worked for me. I keep my vegetable garden fenced at the picket level, about three feet or so. The only time I've seen deer in there is when I leave the gate open.

I did leave the 4' x 4' fence posts at seven feet, in case they changed their minds about hopping in. If that becomes a problem, I'll string the higher fencing along the posts to keep the deer out. My father-in-law says it looks like a cemetery, but that's OK as long as I can pick at the end of the season.

Electric Fencing

This is also a great option. The solar powered version sure makes life easier as far as wiring goes and it works against many pests.

Groundhogs: a Special Case

And speaking of other pests, it's almost impossible to have a garden when a groundhog is in the area. If you live in a part of the country that's never seen a groundhog, count yourself lucky, at least as far as gardens are concerned. I've battled them for a decade in my current garden and use a few techniques to keep them at bay.

I don't have it in my heart to kill them – that's the city boy in me. If they become a nuisance, I use a live trap from Havahart. Baited with apples and peanut butter, it usually only takes a couple of days until I catch the groundhog.

When trapping any animal it's important to check the trap once or twice a day; you don't want the poor thing to suffer in there. Some animals can injure themselves trying relentlessly to escape.

I take them out in the country or to a park and let them go. I know displacing them is not the best thing for them, but it's either that or no garden – and I want to garden.

One summer I had already caught a few groundhogs and released them elsewhere than in my garden. Then came the morning when I got the patriarch of the family, an old mean dude who was not in a mood to be caged up in the trap. As I carried the trap to the truck, he lunged repeatedly towards me. I realized I need to calm him down by covering the trap with a cloth, but that didn't do much.

I put the trap into the back of the truck and headed to a friend's house. We were going to the park to play tennis. He rolled his eyes as he glanced into the bed and saw the groundhog. He mumbled something like, "You gardeners are something else."

I'd never seen anyone else at this park, so I thought it was the perfect place to let Mr. Mean go free. You see, one thing about releasing groundhogs out of a trap is they are very wary. Open the trap and they just sit in there. Poke them with a stick to get them to the open end and they just turn on you.

So here's how I do it when it's time to let them go: I open the trap and secure the door so it can't close, and then I just leave the trap in the back of the truck until the groundhog sneaks out in his own time.

So there's my truck, backed up into the woods, trap open waiting for the groundhog to walk out at his own pace – when a woman shows up with bunch of kids.

Now I'm off a ways playing tennis, but I'm watching as the kids start on the swings to my right (my truck is off to the left). Slowly but surely, the kids start to meander to the left towards the meanest groundhog I've ever seen, that was at that moment cornered in a small cage and not a little annoyed.

After missing badly on a top spin forehand, I stopped, raised both arms and yelled, "Ma'am – there's a groundhog in that truck!" This brought a puzzled look from the woman, then she yelled at the kids to get back to the swings. I walked over to the truck and saw Mr. Mean had taken a powder and I gave the all clear. She took her kids and left.

I've been telling that story for a while now, and because of it I got some great advice from the Humane Society about dealing with groundhogs.

Groundhog-Proof Fencing

The Humane Society has an innovative fencing technique that will keep the varmint out of the garden. Using 36-inch-high chicken wire, bend 12 inches of it at a 90-degree angle at the base of a fence post and bury it a couple of inches underground. The groundhog will dig down until he reaches the bent wire under the surface, and give up.

Leave the top 24 inches unattached to the post, so when the groundhog tries to climb the chicken wire the fence will start to fall back and the groundhog will let go, run away embarrassed and hopefully head for the neighbor's garden, never to return again.

Note: That same fence will work perfectly against rabbits that are hungry for the basil plants and tomato seedlings.

If fencing just isn't an option, there are a slew of products on the market that deter the big three of deer, groundhogs and rabbits. Check online or at your garden center. I like to mix the products up, using two or three over the season in case the pest gets used to the smell or taste of one or the other.

And Then There's Max

Honestly though, the greatest deterrent I've ever had against these pests is my dog Max. He's a mutt who was supposed to be part Lab and part St. Bernard. He's actually looks like a skinny pit bull, a real Heinz 57, but he's fast and protective of his property.

His shoulders are less than three feet off the ground, but he'll sprint toward deer, sending them into a panic. Max returns with his head held high, prancing with pride at defending his territory. How a little dog like that has the guts to chase a deer that could easily stomp and kill him, but still be afraid of our cat, is one of the mysteries of nature.

11

For the Love of Old Tools

Gardens are a form of autobiography.
— Sydney Eddison, *Horticulture* magazine

A quick word about garden tools: Always buy the best you can afford. Take my advice and hopefully you'll be proud to pass down your garden tools to your grandchildren.

I actually still use many of my grandfather's tools in the garden. They won't last forever, but I do some routine maintenance to keep them going for as long as possible.

When they finally bite the dust, I use them in the vegetable garden as ornamentation; it's not for everyone, but my garden is for me.

The old handles of my grandfather's tools were made of tight ash (something that might go the way of the chestnut if we don't find a way to combat the emerald ash borer). I could never replace those handles with the same quality of wood as the originals, so I want to keep them preserved for as long as possible.

I treat them with boiled linseed oil, wiping on the oil with a rag a couple times a year. This keeps the wood moist and helps keep it in good shape. One time, while speaking to a garden club, I mentioned I used boiled linseed oil for this purpose. A man raised his hand and asked, "How long do you boil it for?" I had to laugh as I explained it was just bought as boiled linseed oil.

The metal parts I treat with a thin layer of 30-weight motor oil to help ward off rust. In my tool shed I have a five-gallon bucket filled with play sand. Added to that is a quart of the same oil. When I come in from the garden I just put my shovel into the bucket. The oil coats the shovel and the sand helps clean off any loose dirt.

I used my grandfather's Solid Shank True Temper Lightweight Bantam shovel for years in the vegetable garden. It was smaller than most shovels, perfect for working around the paths of the beds. I knew it was on its last legs when I'd hear the handle creak as I was working in the garden. I only used it for light duty, but when a garden job called for a rock to be pried out of the soil, the rock won, and I was left holding one half of the handle.

I solemnly found a place for it in the vegetable garden with the other broken tools. All summer, that shovel sat in the garden looking ridiculous, just the neck sticking out of the soil. Then I started thinking: As long as the metal part was solid, why not just replace the handle? I looked online for information. But instructions about filing off the rivets don't help much when the rivets are pounded flat.

So I called on my neighbor, Rob Joswiak, who was born with a level in one hand and a drill in the other. "Why don't you just buy a new shovel?" he asked. "I've been down this road before. It's going to cost you just as much to buy the handle." When I explained my sentimental reasons, he offered to help.

I tried my best to pin the shovelhead to the seat of a picnic bench while he drilled and hammered at the stubborn 70-year-old rivets. I hung on as the vibrations shook my hands.

After removing the rivets, he tried drilling and prying out the wood, without much success. He decided to burn it out. Into his soapstone wood burner the shovel went. Twenty minutes later, he pulled it out of the fire and tapped the neck on the bricks and a shower of hot coals tumbled out.

My grandfather's shovel was ready for a new handle. I took it with me to the store to find one that fit. Once home, I pounded it into the head, drilled a couple of holes and hammered in the new rivets. For less than $9, I had resurrected my grandfather's shovel.

I'd do it again in a heartbeat. You don't find tools like that anymore. Or so it seems to me. I never knew my grandfather, but his legacy lives on in my garden with an assortment of his tools, some for working and other just for looking at.

A gardener's tools can be beautiful and sentimental objects. But they should also remind us that it's important to clean up the garden, turn over the beds and cover them with mulch at the end of the season.

Part III

TOMATOES

∿

A world devoid of tomato soup, tomato sauce, tomato ketchup and tomato paste is hard to visualize...How did the Italians eat spaghetti before the advent of the tomato?
– Elizabeth David, *An Omelette and a Glass of Wine*

Tomatoes, garlic and basil grown at Yarnick's Farm.

12

TOMATO FAVORITES

What's in a name?
– SHAKESPEARE, *ROMEO AND JULIET*

Everyone has their favorites when it comes to tomatoes. In fact, it's one of the things that confounds beginners: How do you decide what to grow when there are thousands of varieties to choose from?

Heirlooms are a big part of my tomato garden, but there are plenty of hybrids in there too. I'm not a snob when it comes to heirlooms; I love all tomatoes and I'm always willing to try something that's sent to me.

One of the things I love about being a garden writer is that gardeners will send me seeds of their favorites. I love surprises. Each year I throw a few of these seeds in, only to be subbed out the next season with someone else's favorite.

Have I ever found one tomato this way that I just had to have the next year? Not yet, but there are always new varieties to try and it's fun to see what each garden produces.

Over many years and many experiments, I've concluded that there are some tomatoes that are mandatory for me each season. Here's my list, in order of pure tomato pleasures. Feel free to crib from it until you develop your own.

'Sungold'

Number 1 on my list is 'Sungold' – not an heirloom, but a hybrid. (For a full definition of hybrid, see Chapter 25.) It's also my wife's favorite tomato of all time. It produces hundreds, maybe thousands, of half-inch orange cherry tomatoes that are sweet as sugar. It's a very early tomato and keeps putting on fruit all the way up to frost.

The only downside to this tomato is that it has a tendency to crack, especially after a couple of late-season soaking rains.

'Sun Sugar'

The cracking problem is why I've been trialing 'Sun Sugar.' I have found it to be as sweet as 'Sungold,' but in a different way – maybe a little more fruit. It's very crack resistant, but it will take a couple of seasons to see how it stands up overall with 'Sungold.' These things take time. (My rule is: Before an all-time favorite can be supplanted, it must be soundly thrashed over a period of at least three seasons.)

Then there's the nostalgia factor that plays tricks on me. I become attached to different plants for one reason or another. I can look at those 'Sungold's and be reminded of my wife's sweet smile or deeply tanned skin. 'Sun Sugar' has its work cut out for it, that's for sure. 'Sun Sugar' is very sweet, but doesn't have the slight acidic tomato-like bite that 'Sungold' offers.

So far 'Sun Sugar' is a great tomato. I might just have to grow both. Why not?

'Brandy Boy'

I've been preaching about heirlooms for the last 10 years, but my next favorite "must" in the garden is, ironically, another hybrid.

'Brandy Boy' was a creation from Burpee that changed the seed industry. For the most part, much of the breeding done to tomatoes was for the big guys in commercial production. They needed a tomato that shipped well (thick skin), and ripened all at the same time for a one-time harvest.

With the heirloom boom of the late 1990's, Burpee took the best known heirloom tomato, 'Brandywine,' and bred it with another tomato (which is a secret) to create 'Brandy Boy.' Although fans of its parent don't think 'Brandy Boy' has the same flavor as 'Brandywine,' it's pretty close. The tomato is more vigorous, sets more reliably and ripens sooner.

I love it. The meaty pink beefsteak sets in trusses of three and the blossoms aren't bothered by heat or humidity (whereas, 'Brandywine' has a tendency to drop blossoms and not set fruit in those conditions).

*   *   *

There's more hybrids to talk about later, but we'd better get to the heirlooms now.

✀ SHE COMES IN COLORS ✀

The lure of heirlooms tomatoes is how I discovered that there's more to life than red tomatoes. I was fascinated by orange, purple, white and even tomatoes that are ripe while they're green.

> ✀ Look for my green tomato recipes on pages 87, 88 and 101 — including the calorie-busting but delicious Fried Green Tomatoes.

Getting a visitor to pop a 'Snow White Cherry' tomato in their mouth for the first time might take some doing, especially for children. There is a thrill watching their faces as the little tomatoes explode in their mouth and they taste that sweet flavor for the first time.

> Eating only red tomatoes is like drinking just one type of wine. Every variety of tomato has its own special texture and flavor that should be savored.

I realized how intense my obsession with tomatoes had become when I could actually name the different varieties randomly stored in a huge bowl in the fridge. That was scary.

Most people say that refrigerating tomatoes ruins them, but I love them cold with a little ranch dressing. Meaty, pink tomatoes are some of my favorites; to me they convey the old-fashioned fruit at its best. But as I've discovered new varieties, I've started to favor purple and black tomatoes for their wonderful, complex taste.

Here are some heirlooms I recommend for your enjoyment:

'Cherokee Purple'

One of my favorite's has to be 'Cherokee Purple.' I first heard about it from Tom Hauch at Heirloom Seeds. He described it as a strong tasting tomato, and he was right. Even though I had dabbled with 'Pruden's Purple,' I never really threw myself into the purple and darker tomatoes until I found 'Cherokee Purple.' It's a mid-season, baseball-sized tomato that's vigorous, productive and has a wonderful flavor. Describing it is hard, but once you cross the threshold into the wonderful world of purple, you'll understand this one is a winner.

'Limbaugh Legacy Potato Top'

I couldn't have a tomato garden without 'Limbaugh Legacy Potato Top' tomato (see Chapter 13 for this story about Fred Limbaugh and his superb tomato). Fred introduced me to this great heirloom and the world has kept it viable since the year 2000.

It's a huge (one to three pound) pink tomato with a thin skin, meaty flesh and very few seeds. It's the epitome of old-fashioned, wonderful taste. The downside is that it's very susceptible to blossom drop and is the last tomato to be picked in the fall – but well worth the wait.

'Japanese Black Trifele'

The name alone was enough to get me to try. I can't remember where I found it, but back then it was an unknown. When I dropped a bunch of plants off at Mildreds' (that's correct) Daughter's Farm, which is the last working farm in the Pittsburgh city limits, the folks there were intrigued. Of all the plants I left there,

'Polish Linguista' tomatoes are the long tomatoes above (along with an unnamed heirloom). Prolific, tasty and a great sauce tomato, it dates back to the 1800's.

'White Wonder' tomato. A surprising and tasty treat, this is a mild, sweet tomato that keeps its texture even when it gets big.

Heirlooms at a farmers market. One of the wonderful things about heirlooms is the variety of colors, sizes and shapes.

this one was their favorite. It produces pear-shaped four-ounce tomatoes that have a unique taste. The plant puts on tons of tomatoes and they also store pretty well at the end of the season.

'Rose de Berne'

I discovered 'Rose de Berne' in the garden of Mindy Schwartz, who runs Garden Dreams in Wilkinsburg, Pa. She grows nearly 100 different tomatoes and this one stood out. She walked me through her jungle of plants and picked a pinkish tomato about the size of a tennis ball. When I bit into it I was taken by the acidic old-fashioned flavor – love at first taste.

'Eva Purple Ball'

'Eva Purple Ball' was introduced to me by Stewart Neil when I went to see his heirloom-filled garden in 1997. He lived in Medina, Ohio, and said if he had to pick one tomato, this would be the one. It produces pink tomatoes a little smaller than baseballs. When perfectly ripe, they fall off the vine. It's a wonderful surprise to see one on the ground when visiting the garden in the morning. It's meaty and tasty, definitely one of my favorites.

'Marglobe'

I also have a soft spot in my heart for 'Marglobe,' it's one of the first tomatoes I grew and saved seeds from. Productive, with a sharp acidic taste, this one will never let you down.

'Matt's Wild Cherry'

'Matt's Wild Cherry' puts on thousands of tiny cherry tomatoes – no exaggeration. I was attracted to it because one of my sons is named Matt. Every time I pick a fruit from these plants I think of the good times we had together when he was little.

'Pineapple'

I was so thrilled when my in-laws Pat and Don Righi embraced the heirloom tomatoes I gave them one season. When Cindy and I visited for Christmas they had saved the little tags that came with the plants, so they could be sure to get the same varieties next year.

One of their favorites was 'Pineapple,' that they grew in a pot. It's a big tomato, up to two pounds – yellow with red streaks. It's got a unique taste and meaty texture. There's something exciting about turning the people you love onto the things you love in the garden.

'Stupice'

One of the best early heirloom tomatoes is 'Stupice.' It produces small, two-ounce tomatoes that are sometimes round, but also can be irregular shaped. It's very productive and puts on its tasty fruit early and keeps putting on tomatoes until frost.

'Fourth of July'

'Fourth of July' is a hybrid that is early and productive. I love this variety not just for its earliness, but also its prolific nature and great tasting tomatoes.

'Juliet'

'Juliet' is bigger than a grape tomato, but smaller than a normal sauce tomato. It's another hybrid, vigorous and extremely productive. This 1999 All America Selection is one of my favorites for its sheer determination in producing tomatoes. This one needs to be fully ripe to get the best taste. Pick it early and you'll wonder what all the fuss is about, wait until it's deep red and you'll see why this one is a winner.

'Pink Oxheart'

I can't think of a tomato that tastes better than 'Pink Oxheart.' But it's not for everyone. Gardeners used to juicy tomatoes might not appreciate the meaty texture of 'Pink Oxheart' and other tomatoes like it. To me, these tomatoes are nirvana.

✂ FOND MEMORIES OF HYBRID TOMATOES PAST ✂

Some of my favorite hybrids unfortunately have gone out of favor and can no longer be found. That's one of the problems about getting sucked into the hybrids; you have to rely on a company to keep selling it. If it doesn't sell, it's out of the catalog.

The one I miss the most is Burpee's **'Pixie II'**, purely for the memories. It was one of my first and favorites for containers. When I think of 'Pixie II' I think of Pam, one of my dearest and oldest friends. She was an intern for me back in the 1980's at the Medina County *Gazette*. I hired her full time, and followed her to the *Pittsburgh Post-Gazette*.

This farm girl lived in an apartment in the city of Medina when she was working there and I brought her a couple of the 'Pixie II' plants. She put them in five-gallon containers and tended them all summer, harvesting great bunches of the two-inch fruits. I'm sure there's something newer, better, earlier and more prolific, but I just want 'Pixie II' back for the memories.

Another that's no longer around came from Park Seed, called **'Container Choice.'** Bred to grow in pots, it produced beefsteak tomatoes that tasted like a summer tomato should. I grow **'Super Bush'** now, and I like it, but I always thought 'Container Choice' was something special.

Each season brings new tomatoes to my garden from friends and readers. Some of these gift plants are great and stick around for decades, others are forgotten, enjoying the spotlight for a season or two until they fade away.

It's hard to navigate all the different types of tomatoes out there and it's best just to look around and find your own favorites.

Just because I like these tomatoes doesn't mean you will. Use the list as a starting point for a lifetime learning experience. There are literally thousands of different varieties out there to try, so dig up another patch of earth, improve it with compost and give something that sounds interesting a try.

I often fantasize about having enough land to try two of every tomato I can find. Kind of like a Noah in the garden, walking from row to row tasting different varieties, figuring out what was earliest, biggest and best. That would be a dream come true for me. But fantasy and reality are two different things. Could you imagine what it would take to care for 500 plants, 1000 plants?

I've often thought of finding a piece of land with lots of sun and planting everything, and I do mean everything. In between those rows of tomatoes would be every different type of garlic known to man. The tomatoes would be sold at farmers markets and the garlic to other home growers.

The farm would also be a place for gardeners to learn how to grow. Throw in a few young, fresh-faced, enthusiastic interns and I think you'd have something.

Sounds romantic doesn't it – until there's too much rain or not enough, and there's pests, diseases, thieves and exhaustion.

Even so, sounds like the perfect retirement to me: turning people onto heirlooms and growing things the right way. I guess we can all dream.

Tomato Varieties for Quick Reference

NAME	COLOR	DESCRIPTION
'Sungold'	Orange	Small, sweet prolific cherry with zing; my wife's favorite tomato
'Sun Sugar'	Orange	Like 'Sungold,' doesn't crack as much, sweet but no zing.
'Brandy Boy'	Pink	Bred from 'Brandywine.' Sooner, more reliable, prolific and tasty.
'Cherokee Purple'	Dark red	Wonderful flavor, reliable setter.
'Limbaugh Legacy Potato Top'	Pink	Old-fashioned flavor, big, thin- skinned tomato. Blossom drop in high heat.
'Japanese Black Trifele'	Dark red	Medium-sized pear-shaped tomatoes, prolific and special flavor.
'Rose de Berne'	Pink	Tennis-ball-sized and a winner for flavor.
'Eva Purple Ball'	Pink	Falls off vine when ripe, superior taste, disease resistant.
'Marglobe'	Red	Old-fashioned favorite, acidic in a good way.
'Matt's Wild Cherry'	Red	Thousands of small, sweet cherry tomatoes.
'Pineapple'	Dark yellow and orange	Big, multi-colored, beautiful and meaty.
'Stupice'	Red	Two ounce irregular-shaped early tomato.
'Fourth of July'	Red	Early, prolific, long-lasting and flavorful.
'Juliet'	Red	Lots of tomatoes between grape and Roma size. Must be completely ripe to enjoy flavor.
'Pink Oxheart'	Pink	Large heart-shaped meaty tomato with old-fashioned sweet flavor.

Simple Perfect Tomato Sandwich

Nothing can compare to a big meaty beefsteak tomato combined with garlic, basil, olive oil, cheese and bread. It's a simple thing that is so good because the ingredients are. Get a cold beer, glass of good wine, or tall iced tea and go sit out in the garden with your sandwich and watch the plants grow.

What You Need:

2 pieces white bread or good Italian bread
2 cloves fresh garlic, minced
2 tablespoons olive oil
1 good, tasty, large tomato

1 stalk of basil
1 oz. buffalo mozzarella cheese
Sea salt to taste
Fresh ground pepper to taste

Here's How:

Toast the bread (if it's white bread, use a toaster; if it's Italian bread, put it under the broiler until golden brown).

On a cutting board, combine the minced garlic with the olive oil. Add the basil and a pinch or two of sea salt and some pepper. Chop and blend with a sharp knife or, better yet, put the mixture into a mortar and pestle.

Make a paste out of the ingredients and spread it on the bread.

Slice the cheese and lay that over the paste, then top it off with sliced tomato.

Serves 1.

Simple Red Sauce

Sauces don't get any easier than this, and they don't get much better either. This one's bound to be a trusty stand-by for almost any occasion, but it's especially good for summer.

Take special note of Chef Donato Coluccio's exploding garlic technique. He taught me this and now I use it for most of my garlic dishes. (Donato is executive chef at Pittsburgh's Capital Grille.)

What You Need:

2 tablespoons good-quality olive oil
10 cloves garlic
½ cup chicken stock

4 large tomatoes, with seeds and peels, cubed
1 cup chopped basil
salt and pepper, to taste

Here's How:

Heat two tablespoons of good olive oil on medium high heat. Slice 5 garlic cloves, and mince the other 5. Add the sliced garlic cloves to the oil and cook for a minute. Then add the minced garlic cloves and cook for another 30 seconds. Immediately add the cold chicken stock – this stops the garlic from cooking any longer.

Now, I don't peel my tomatoes or remove the seeds. I think they're an important addition to a summer sauce, and good in other uses too.

Lower the heat, add the cubed tomatoes and cook for 5 minutes.

Remove from heat and add a cup of chopped basil. Add salt and pepper to taste and you have an easy, delicious red sauce.

13

"THE BEST TOMATO YOU'VE EVER TASTED"

There can be no other occupation like gardening in which, if you were to creep up behind someone at their work, you would find them smiling.
— MIRABEL OSLER

The 'Limbaugh Legacy Potato Top' tomato is named for my friend Fred Limbaugh who lived in Robinson, Pennsylvania, when I met him.

He called me at work one day in 2000 at the *Pittsburgh Post-Gazette* and told me he grew "the best tomato you've ever tasted." I rolled my eyes sitting at my desk, but Fred convinced me to come out to his home and get a few plants.

I prided myself on my growing prowess in the greenhouse until I saw the plants Fred had for me. They were deep green compared to the pale shade of the tomatoes I was growing. His were two feet high, with stems as thick as my thumb.

Fred told me of the rich history of this tomato, how his father and grandfather had grown them and how he continued the tradition. In the 1930's Fred took the tomatoes around his neighborhood, selling them to eager customers. They were that good, he told me.

He worked as a streetcar conductor, then drove buses, and along the way he'd meet people who wanted to try this great tomato. Every year he grew hundreds of new plants on his windowsill, then he'd take them down a steep hill to his cold frames, where they would stay until planting time.

I took the two plants he gave me and planted them with the other 50 types I was growing at the time. At the end of the season I realized Fred was right. His plants produced huge (one to three pound) pink, thin-skinned tomatoes with few seeds. They tasted like heaven.

I wondered, though, what would happen when Fred, who was in his 80's wouldn't be able to grow these tomatoes anymore. One night while lying in bed, I had an inspiration: I'd give some seeds away to readers and then they could grow the tomato out and send back the seeds, providing more for next season and spreading the variety – insuring it never becomes extinct.

I had my doubters that first year. The bosses at the paper allowed me to run the project, but warned me that, human nature being what it is, once I sent the seeds out in the required SASE, that'd be the last I'd hear from the gardeners, because everyone just wants something for free.

Well, one year we got 140,000 seeds back. You see, gardeners aren't like most people; they love to be part of something, to perpetuate something wonderful like 'Limbaugh Legacy Potato Top.'

Over the years, Fred would call me and laugh at how popular the tomato had become. It started to be grown all over the world after word got out on the Internet. He was never one for the limelight, but was just proud that his family's heritage tomato might live forever.

I'd stop by when I was out and have a beer with him at his house and share gardening stories while his beloved German shepherd looked on. After his health started to go, I'd visit him at his retirement home. He was figuring out a way to grow tomatoes on a windowsill there, too, so he could still provide plants for everyone who asked. For my part, I'd grow out as many plants as possible for him so he could continue to give them away. I was embarrassed by the scrawny plants I provided when I'd meet his daughter Pat at Fred's house and give her a few flats of the tomatoes.

Fred passed away in 2008. He was 86. He'd been out the night before with his family and then was gone early the next morning.

I always felt we were kindred spirits whose love of gardening transcended the boundaries of age. I'll never forget that first day we met, when he gave me those two large plants, their roots surrounded with newspaper.

I miss Fred. I think of him as I sit at home filling the thousands of seed envelopes to be sent to gardeners around the world. It feels good knowing that his name will always be linked to a family heirloom that will live on in gardens around the world.

The most ironic thing about Fred, though, was that he didn't even like tomatoes – he just grew them for the rest of us. Now that's a true gardener.

Compared to the predictable beauty of hybrid tomatoes, heirloom tomatoes might be called ugly, but they can be the tastiest of all.

Readers of my garden column line up on a Sunday afternoon for my heirloom tomato plant giveaway in front of the *Post-Gazette*.

14

THE KID IN THE TOMATO SUIT

I'll try anything once.
— RICHARD PETTY

Tomatoes have always played a big role in our family. The first year of my obsession I decided to do a public giveaway of the 'Limbaugh Legacy Potato Top" tomato plants I'd been nurturing. I put a small blurb in my column to that effect. I was going to do it on a Sunday, downtown, right in front of the *Pittsburgh Post-Gazette* building.

I figured, first off, if no one came there would be no loss, and secondly, if we did it on a Sunday, there's free street parking and no traffic.

I wanted something special for the event and thought that if I had someone to walk around dressed as a tomato, I'd get some attention right off. So I went to a costume shop to see if I could find a tomato costume. The closest I got was an orange pumpkin, but I figured with some spray paint and a little imagination I'd have a tomato.

A half hour and a can of red spray paint later I had my tomato; now I had to find someone to wear it. My search was fruitless until I waved a twenty-dollar bill in front of my then twelve-year-old son Matt's face.

Sunday came, and I crossed my fingers that people would actually be interested in coming downtown to get a free heirloom tomato.

As Matt and I sat up in the second floor of the building waiting for the event to start, I got a call from security at the front desk. They informed me that there was a line around the block and that even though we weren't supposed to start for a half hour, we better get down there and start giving away plants.

My 12-year-old son Matt as 'Tomato Boy' – it was his first and last time in a tomato suit.

Matt was the hit of the event in his blue sneakers, baseball hat and giant red tomato suit, as I put my flats of tomatoes up on the large mail boxes outside the building and gave away plants to the patient gardeners in line.

That was the last time I was able to convince my son to do anything that silly again; he soon became too cool or too smart to participate in such activities. Every once a while I'll stumble onto a picture of Matt in his tomato suit with a sweet smile on his face. Smiling all the way to the bank.

I've still got that big tomato, which has faded back to orange, hanging in my closet. Maybe one day I'll be able to find someone to wear it. I've got a feeling it's going to cost me more than twenty bucks.

A couple of years later, I landed a radio show with my co-host Jessica Walliser, called "The Organic Gardeners." We had an early Sunday morning time slot and my kids never heard the show. For them, Sunday was for sleeping in.

On Father's Day we got a call from "MJ", a listener who was having problems with his tomato plants. He said that he would see his tomatoes in the morning, but something would get them during the day, and did I have any suggestions as to what could be eating them?

My first guess was groundhogs, since they feed in the daylight hours. I asked a few more questions and the caller finally admitted he knew what was taking the tomatoes; it was his father.

Jess started laughing and said, "That's your son, Matt."

I didn't have a clue, but the fact that as a teenager, he drug himself out of bed on a Sunday morning meant the world to me.

I love that the garden is intertwined with our lives and helps us recall the evolution of a young family.

15

THE 'MORTGAGE LIFTER' TOMATO
(AND A BRIEF HOW-TO ABOUT CROSS-BREEDING)

The greatest service which can be rendered any country
is to add a useful plant to its culture.
— THOMAS JEFFERSON

I'd heard the story of the **'Mortgage Lifter'** tomato a thousand times, but just like the old telephone game, the story had changed over the years and I had it wrong.

Marshall Cletis Byles was the man who created the tomato and his grandson Ed Martin of Virginia had the foresight to record his grandfather's story when the old man was in his 80's.

Here's the Story...

Marshall Cletis despised his given names and chose to go by Charlie, or just M.C. M.C. worked as an auto mechanic in West Virginia. His shop was at the bottom of a long road that wound up a mountain, and when trucks would blow their radiator they'd roll back down to Charlie's shop. That's where people think he got his other name, Radiator Charlie.

It's funny, but the way I always heard (and told) the story, his shop was at the top of the hill, and when the trucks would lose their radiator they would stop on top to get the work done. I like M.C.'s version better.

M.C. might have been a mechanic, but he was also a man who tried to make a better tomato – without a day of school under his belt and certainly no plant breeding experience.

Sometime in the 1940s he took 10 plants with the biggest seeds he could find and he circled them around a '**German Johnson**' tomato plant. When those 10 plants blossomed, he collected the pollen with a baby's ear syringe and carefully put it into the flowers of the 'German Johnson.'

He saved seeds from that plant and continued planting them for seven years until he finally found a tomato with the characteristics he wanted. That was the first and last plant breeding he ever did.

Back then, a dollar was a lot to pay for a plant, but that's what M.C. sold his new tomato plant for. People were willing to pay and he sold a lot of them. In just six years, Charlie raised $6000 and paid off the mortgage on his house.

The tomato is still readily available in many catalogs. Radiator Charlie's 'Mortgage Lifter' has been a favorite of gardeners for decades. It's a huge tomato, anywhere from two to four pounds when grown in good soil. The plants are very productive and resist diseases. The fruit is slightly flattened, pinkish red, meaty and filled with old-fashioned flavor.

✄ EASY TIPS FOR CROSS-BREEDING TOMATOES ✄

Maybe you'd like to create your own variety of tomato by crossing your favorites and seeing what happens.

The technique isn't much different today than it was back in Radiator Charlie's time. The distance between tomatoes makes no difference since the flowers are self-pollinating. The only reason I can think Charlie formed the circle was so that it was easy to get from one plant to the other with the pollen.

First off, this is the type of thing that needs records, so be sure to record what you're doing, when you're doing it and who's crossing with whom.

You're going to be creating a new variety of tomato by combining the pollen of two different plants.

Step 1 – Prepping Your Plants

Find a yellow tomato flower that hasn't opened yet. If it has, chances are the flower already pollinated itself. In that case, move onto another flower.

You'll get the hang of it after you take a look at the flowers; they should show yellow just before opening.

The anther cone is sticking out of the petals. Pinch the side of the cone with tweezers and, holding the base of the flower, pull straight out. You're removing the anther cone to expose something called the stigma, so you can get to it and put some pollen on it. The anther cone is discarded. You have to be careful not to damage the other parts of the flower (you can practice on flowers that have already opened).

The exposed stigma is not ready to receive the pollen yet; it will become sticky in another day or so. At this point, I like to gently cover the flower with a floating row cover to be sure other pollinators don't get to it overnight. Gently is the key word here.

Tomato seeds that I started in the greenhouse.

Step 2 – Pollinating

Now go to the plant that will be donating the pollen to your prepared plant and remove the anther cones from opened or partially opened flowers. Let the anthers dry out and put them on a piece of glass. They will release the pollen; keep it cool until you're ready to cross. Sometimes you can tap it out of the dried anthers; some people use an electric toothbrush.

Take a small, fine paintbrush and transfer the donor pollen to the sticky stigma of the flower to receive it. Use lots of pollen, but be gentle. You'll know if the cross takes when a small fruit develops in several days.

Once there's a fruit on the crossed plant, mark it immediately; that's where you'll harvest the tomatoes at the end of the season. That seed will be what you created by the cross.

Step 3 – Watching and Waiting

Now comes the hard work of figuring out if the variety you've created is any good and will reliably come true (meaning, it will replicate itself consistently).

Next season, plant as many of the seeds as possible. You'll need a good test group to record how they do. Watch which plant has the traits you long for: whether it's the biggest, earliest, tastiest, disease resistant or all of the above. Keeping careful records is a must.

Repeat this for several seasons until you've got something you love that makes the same thing each year.

Name it after me, if you don't mind. I'd love to have a variety that would outlive me.

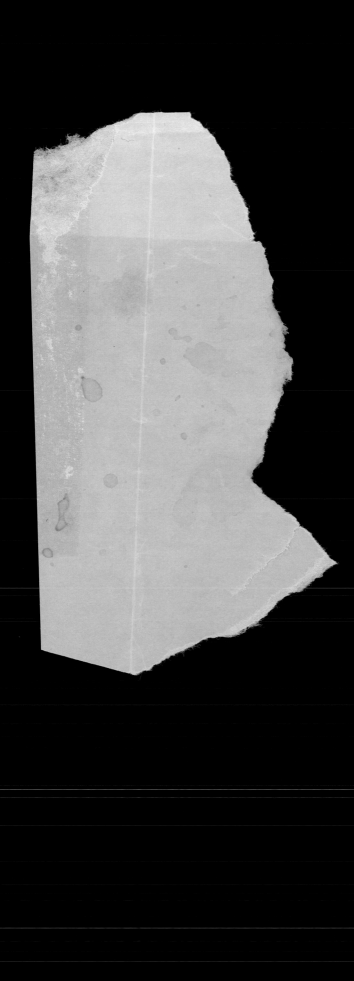

Green Tomato Pie

This is another one of those pies that makes a meal. There's sweetness, spice and tanginess here, but it all works together perfectly. Use those end-of-season green tomatoes and take a chance on this unusual but easy recipe. I'll bet you'll be glad you did.

What You Need:

1 pre-made or homemade double pie crust
  (pie dough with a top and a bottom)
2 cups chopped green tomatoes
½ cup brown sugar
2 teaspoons white vinegar
½ teaspoon cinnamon

½ cup chopped raisins
4 tablespoon melted butter
½ teaspoon salt
¼ teaspoon ground cloves
⅛ teaspoon nutmeg

Here's How:

Preheat oven to 375°F.

Place the chopped green tomatoes in a pot of water, cover and bring to a boil.

Drain, add the other filling ingredients, and mix.

Place the pie dough in a pie pan if it isn't in one already, and fill with the tomato mix. Cover with the pie dough piece and make 2 or 3 slashes in the middle with a knife.

Crimp the edge with your fingers, all the way around.

Bake for about 40 minutes or until the crust is golden brown.

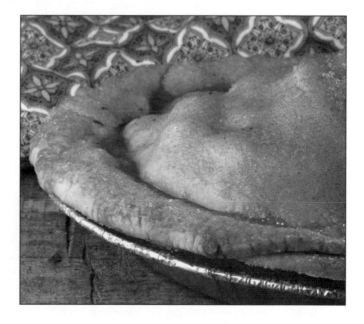

Fried Green Tomatoes

This is a classic old recipe that's the perfect dish for the end of the season. There's something about the combination of spicy breading and tart fruit that is irresistible. Green tomatoes are just what they sound like: not quite ripe. So eating fried green tomatoes is a leap of faith, but once you try them, you'll see, you can't get enough. Not the healthiest way to eat vegetables, but once or twice a year, why not?

At the end of the season there are always lots of leftover green tomatoes. I save them and hope they'll ripen through the late fall and early winter. But many of them never turn; they stay bright green, young and firm.

What You Need:

3 medium-sized, firm green tomatoes
½ cup all-purpose flour
1 teaspoon hot pepper flakes
(if you like it spicy)
¼ cup milk

2 beaten eggs
²/₃ cup fine dry bread crumbs or cornmeal
¼ cup olive oil
½ teaspoon salt
¼ teaspoon pepper

Here's How:

Cut unpeeled tomatoes into ½ inch slices. Sprinkle slices with salt, pepper and hot pepper flakes. Let tomato slices absorb the spices for a half hour.

Place the flour, milk and eggs in three separate shallow containers. Place the bread crumbs in a fourth shallow container.

Heat 4 tablespoons of olive oil in a skillet on medium-high heat.

Dip tomatoes in milk, then flour, then eggs, then bread crumbs. In the skillet, fry half of the coated tomato slices at a time, for 5 to 7 minutes on each side, or until brown. Add olive oil as needed while frying up the rest of the tomatoes.

Season to taste with salt and pepper, and enjoy.

Serves 4.

16

BASIC TOMATO GROWING

In the spring, at the end of the day, you should smell like dirt.
— MARGARET ATWOOD

I've got an old gardening friend who says, "There's two things money can't buy – true love and homegrown tomatoes." There's a popular song to that effect. Anyone who's stood out in the garden and enjoyed soft, ripe fruit warmed by the sun knows that's true.

Tomatoes are the one crop that just about anyone can grow. It could be a field of 100 different heirlooms or just a few plants on the side of the garage, or in a lone pot on the deck of your condo.

It's All About Sunshine and Good Soil

Regardless of how many tomatoes or what kind of plants are grown, the best results are achieved when they are grown in good soil and in full sun. But if you get less than that much sun, go ahead and plant anyway. In my garden I get only about six hours of direct sun and I still harvest lots of tomatoes. The plants grow tall and leggy, but happily supply us with all the fruit we could ask for (Yes, tomatoes are botanically a fruit, because what they produce has seeds – which makes a pumpkin a fruit as well. Call them whatever you want).

Concerned that you don't have good soil? Guess what? Not many of us do, we just make it better.

If your plants are just limping along, and over on your neighbor's side of the fence you see a jungle of green tomato plants heavy with fruit, you know there's something more you could be doing. In all likelihood, your neighbor will be happy to offer advice for a better crop. Gardeners are like that.

Here's what I'd advise: By adding organic matter – like well-aged animal manure, dehydrated manure, mushroom manure or, best of all, compost – you'll be giving your soil what it needs. And in turn, the plants can take what they want from it. The idea is to have soft, fertile soil. If you're starting with clay or rocky soil, that will take some extra work, but it pays off with a bountiful harvest of tasty fruit.

A Word About Timing

One of the biggest mistakes made in the garden is planting outside too early. Tomatoes love warm soil, and in cool climates that happens when spring turns

Cherry tomatoes like 'Sungold' (right) are a sweet, prolific treat in the garden. 'Sungold' is my wife's favorite and has earned a perpetual place in the garden.

into summer. There are lots of ways to stretch the season on both sides (I'll discuss that later in Chapter 21) but as a rule of thumb, wait to plant until a week or two after the last chance of frost.

When tomatoes are put into the cool spring ground they just sit there and wait until the soil warms up. They won't start putting on tomatoes until nighttime air temperatures stay around 50°F or higher.

✖ KEEPING YOUR PLANTS WARM AND HEALTHY ✖

Mulch

Your tomato plants will be grateful to you if you use mulch. Mulch is something to cover the ground around the plants – straw or compost – and it offers many benefits for gardeners.

Some gardeners put the mulch on when they plant, others like to wait until the soil warms up. There are two thoughts about when to add mulch: Adding mulch early is a technique to battle fungal diseases before they get started. If the fungal spores on the ground can't be splashed up onto the leaves, the plant will stay healthier longer. On the other hand, gardeners who wait to spread mulch are taking advantage of the sun to quickly heat the soil, something tomatoes love.

Black Landscape Fabric

This is my favorite for heating up the soil; you can find it at most good garden centers. The landscape fabric is porous, letting both air and water through. I've used black plastic, but unless there's irrigation underneath, I find the soil becomes too dry by the end of the season. However, red plastic is reputed to help warm the soil and increase yields for tomatoes.

Like most things in gardening, everyone has their own way of doing things. Just because someone writes a book or calls themselves an expert doesn't mean they are the be-all and end-all. If your plants are healthy and fruitful, you're doing something right. And even if you don't end up with the tomatoes of your dreams the first time out, having fun and discovering the wonders of the garden often trumps actual results.

Feed the soil, plant at the right time, use mulch and enjoy yourself. Before you know it, you'll be knee deep in tomatoes begging friends, neighbors, relatives — and occasionally strangers — to take some tomatoes home with them.

17

TOMATO PLANTING TECHNIQUES

*[I] stand in deep contemplation over my vegetable progeny
with a love that nobody could share or conceive of who had never
taken part in the process of creation.*
— NATHANIEL HAWTHORNE, *MOSSES FROM AN OLD MANSE*, 1854

Planting day is the most thrilling and wonderful time in the garden, until your tomatoes are ready to be picked. The garden is fertile, the soil has started to warm and there's no chance of another frost.

There's no "best" way to grow your tomatoes; everyone has a preference. Over the years I've staked them, caged them and even let them crawl prostrate on the ground, and they still perform their delicious miracles for me.

The Hole

I like to dig the planting hole about a foot deep, put two heaping shovelfuls of compost in and then set the plant in the compost. I always plant a little low, to leave a depression to catch as much rain as possible.

Let 'Em Sprawl?

After that, the question becomes how to support the plants, or to support them at all. Letting the vines sprawl wildly along the ground is how tomatoes were meant to grow, and they are very productive when grown this way. The plant doesn't need to expend energy to climb, so in theory it puts on more tomatoes. The long vines will attach roots to the soil, allowing the plant to pull nutrition from its limbs as well, instead of only from the base of the plant.

Being close to the ground, though, has its drawbacks. During a wet season some of the fruit can be lost to rot. With tomatoes closer to the ground, pests have better access to the plants. When left to their own deserts the vines will cover a large area. You may not have the space to spare. I've experimented with growing tomatoes without cages or stakes and liked the results. But since my vegetable garden is only 30' x 40', I've gone back to growing vertically, only because I want to grow more plants.

Partial Support

To keep the plants off the ground I've used wooden pallets when planting. I would get the soil prepared, and then place pallets in the bed. I planted the seedlings (one per pallet) in between the wood slats. As the plants started to roam, I added more pallets. Sometimes the plants became just too big to get into and pick, a good problem to have if you've got plenty of room for the sprawl.

Staking

Staking is probably the most popular way to support tomatoes. Be sure to install the stake immediately after planting. If you wait a couple of weeks to drive in the stake, you could damage the root system. Use something that's at least one inch square and five feet tall.

Staking is time consuming and something that has to be maintained as the plant grows. The plant should also be pruned to one main stem. Use a nice soft flexible tie to attach the plants to the stake (pantyhose are great, and green garden tape

'Green Zebra' tomato is ripe when it develops an orange hue. You may need some prodding to taste one for the first time, but after that the sky's the limit.

works fine too). But be warned: If you don't maintain the staking and go a month or so without tying up the vines, you could find yourself struggling to lift the heavy, brittle vines back onto the stake, and not hurt your plant.

Caging

Because I never can keep up with the plants by careful attention to staking, I'll offer one other option: caging – my favorite way to support the plants. I'm not talking about the tiny support hoops sold in garden stores. They may be good for peppers, but tomato plants will outgrow them in about a month.

I build my own cages out of concrete reinforcing wire. It's what contractors use to pour concrete over. A 25-foot roll is cheap and will make five cages. Here's how: Cut five-foot lengths and attach each end, making a large cylindrical cage that's also five feet high.

When the plants are put in place, lift the cage over them and push it down into the soil. In soft soil, jiggling the cage from left to right will hold it in place. Then, to anchor it firmly, pound a stake into the soil and tie it to the cage; at the end of the season the weight of the vines can tip a cage over without the extra support of a stake.

Even at five feet, the tomatoes will probably need higher support. They do in my garden, because of the lack of sunshine, which makes them reach farther for the light. My tomatoes are planted along a picket fence. The 4' x 4's that support the fence are seven feet high, with a cap. I run a wire across the top of the 4' x 4's and then run twine in a pattern down to the top of the cage. The plants will lie on the string and climb with a little help. At the end of the season, it's a tomato jungle, but that's fine with me.

Staking all'Italiano

Another technique that I've been experimenting with is a staking style I saw in Italy. One set of stakes is driven into the ground in the conventional manner, straight up. Then another stake is attached to the top of the first stake at a

45-degree angle, it looks almost like a teepee or isosceles triangle. A long row of these is installed, every three to five feet. They can also be connected by twine to give the tomatoes more support. The tomatoes are planted at the base of the second stake (see diagram). They will grow along the angle to the top. It looks great, especially with long bamboo stakes. Since the plants are lying at a 45-degree angle, maintaining the vines is not as critical.

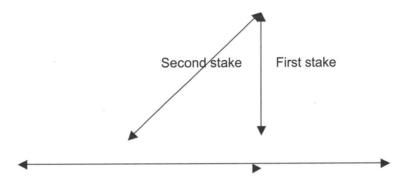

The bottom line represents the ground. This is a side view. The plants are planted at the base of the second stake.

Upside Down in a Bucket

Upside down tomatoes have become quite the rage over the last few years. I first heard about them in 2000 from a reader of my newspaper column in the *Pittsburgh Post-Gazette*. The reader, the late Tom Robinson, had heard about tomatoes growing that way in Florida and as a conversation piece he planted one. After that, he was sold on the method. Tom told me he got tomatoes earlier from the 'Super Bush' variety when it was grown upside down.

His technique is what I use for growing a couple of plants a year upside down. Although there are commercial planters on the market, using a five-gallon plastic bucket like Tom did is a better idea, to my mind; many of those hanging bags you find at the garden centers seem too small, and need to be watered and fertilized more often when the weather gets hot.

So here's how it works: Take the bucket and cut out the two-inch round hole in the bottom. There's already a template there from the process used to make the bucket. Hang the bucket on something sturdy that will hold 20 to 30 pounds. Take your bush or container tomato and push it, roots-first, up through the hole from the bottom; it will be growing upside down from the hole. Reach into the bucket and install a round piece of plastic on the bottom, with a V cut in it. The piece is set into place around the stem of the plant to hold it in place.

You can improvise with almost any kind of plastic. I use the round plastic that comes from the bottom of hanging baskets. It's there to make sure the basket drains, and when I empty out the basket at the end of the season the plastic piece falls out, ready for its second life in my upside down tomato bucket.

Now fill the bucket with something good, like compost mixed 50/50 with planting mix. Pack it pretty tight into the bucket. You'll know it's time to water when you see the leaves start to droop. Keep the soil evenly moist and fertilize at least once a month, and your upside down tomatoes will be the talk of the neighborhood. Tom had another trick that I use for decorative effect: Plant the top of the bucket with flowers. You'll have good things coming and going!

Since tomatoes form roots along their stems, here are some other ways you can plant them, other than conventionally (if you call upside down conventional).

Going Deep

This planting method may work best in warmer climates. First, remove the leaves along the stem, leaving only the top foliage. The plant can then be planted deep, with only the top part poking out of the soil. The plus side to this is that the root ball will stay moist longer when it's planted so deep, but the down side is that it will be cool, and tomatoes thrive in heat.

Going Horizontal

I like to use horizontal trenching on some of my tomatoes. I plant this way when tomatoes get long and leggy during the late spring, when I've been lazy and haven't gotten them into the garden soon enough.

I remove the leaves, except for the top growth, and dig a trench the length of the plant, just a few inches deep. Then I lay the plant on its side and cover the vines with soil – or better yet, compost – all the way up to the top leaves. If you're also staking, drive it in immediately; otherwise, you risk installing the stake right through the stem.

Some of the most prolific plants I've ever grown were planted horizontally. Every year I put a few in this way for fun...even if I haven't been lazy.

✄ CONTAINER PLANTING ✄

Tomato junkies know that eventually there's not enough space in the garden to grow every variety they long for, and they turn to containers. Or it could be that they don't have space for a garden at all, but dream of homegrown tomatoes in a city patio or deck.

The most important part of growing tomatoes in containers is getting the right sized pot – the bigger the better, depending on the growth habits of your plant. It's a good idea, before you start, to know something about the potential size and shape of the plant you have in mind.

There are tomatoes that are called "determinate," meaning they only grow so big and stop – usually to a compact four to five feet – and their fruit ripens over a short period of time. Those are great for growing in pots. You'll find these tomatoes at the nursery labeled as bush tomatoes, patio tomatoes or container tomatoes. 'Super Bush,' the variety I use as an upside down tomato (and Tom Robinson's favorite early tomato) is a wonderful choice for a pot.

Because even a determinate tomato grown in a good potting mix can outgrow its pot and spread a bit, this would be a good candidate for a store-bought tomato cage.

"Indeterminate" is the term used for regular-sized vining tomatoes – the kind that continue to set fruit throughout the season until the frost. Since they are actually vines, they also continue to grow and spread. For these, try to find a pot the size of half a whiskey barrel.

Care and Feeding

Fill the container with compost if you've got enough; if not, find a good organic bagged potting mix filled with nutrients. For a big container I'll also use mulch, to help keep the soil evenly moist. You see, tomatoes are heavy feeders and will need everything possible in the soil to keep them growing strong.

Containers should be fertilized every two weeks to assure that the plants are getting everything they need. It is essential to keep an even moisture. If the pots are allowed to dry out, and then you soak them, thinking you're doing the right thing, *blossom end rot* can rear its ugly head.

Blossom End Rot

Potted plants are more prone to BER because of their watering requirements. The disease is caused by a calcium deficiency; the calcium is usually there in the soil, but the plants just can't get it, due to improper watering.

The rot shows up at the bottom of the tomato as a sunken black area. Some tomatoes are more prone to the rot than others. Sometimes it's only the first tomatoes that are affected and often they will heal themselves when watering is done right.

To find out if a container needs to be watered, just poke a finger down into the soil. If the soil is dry a few inches down, water until it starts to flow out of the bottom of the container. Just do your best not to let it go completely dry. You won't need to be as attentive in May when rain is plentiful, as you will be in July and August when your pots might need to be watered daily. Who said gardening was always going to be easy?

Mine isn't the last word on growing tomatoes, so I hope you'll experiment with different techniques for growing and maybe create your own. It's fun to mix things up and discover what works best for you.

Pickled Green Tomatoes with Garlic

Try these instead of traditional pickles for a sandwich. They'll keep for months.

What You Need:

6 pint-sized jars, suitable for jam or pickling
4 cups white vinegar
2 tablespoons kosher salt or pickling salt
Juice of one lemon
2 tablespoons pickling spice,
  either homemade or store-bought

6 jalapeño peppers
Approx. 60 garlic cloves
4 to 6 pounds green tomatoes,
  peeled and quartered

Here's How:

Clean and sterilize your jars according to the manufacturer's instructions.

Score your tomatoes with an X in the bottom. Plunge them into boiling water for 15 to 30 seconds, then immediately plunge them into ice water to cool. Remove the skin, which should come right off.

In a small saucepan bring the vinegar, salt, lemon juice and pickling spice to a simmer. While waiting for saucepan to simmer, add

about 10 garlic cloves to each jar. Then, add the tomatoes to the jars, up to about ½ inch below the rim.

If you want to use the jalapeños, add them to your jars too.

Strain the simmering liquid into a pitcher with a pour spout and then pour over tomatoes in each jar, to about ¼ from the rim.

Remove all air bubbles with a butter knife.

Wipe rims with a clean damp cloth and screw bands and lids on finger-tight.

Place in a boiling water bath (double boiler) for 40 minutes.

Remove and cool to room temperature. Leave jars alone to seal themselves within 12 hours; if any don't form a good seal, discard those individual jars.

Makes 6 pints, depending on size of tomatoes.

18

THE GARDEN DOG

*Man is rated the highest animal, at least among all animals
who returned the questionnaire.*
— ROBERT BRAULT

My first "off colored" tomato I grew was 'Pruden's Purple.' It was also the first heirloom I'd ever grown. I came to know this wonderful tomato in a roundabout way: I'd gotten some pole bean seeds from a guy I did a story on when I was working at the Medina County *Gazette*. Bob Janca was one of the first people I ever ran into who were growing heirlooms in the 80's. He gave me a small packet of 'Cherokee Trail of Tears' beans. I fell in love with that pole bean and it's still my favorite to this day. It's got an amazing nutty flavor and it's prolific. I sent some off to Johnny's Selected Seeds to see if they might want to carry them in their catalog.

The nice people at Johnny's sent me back some seeds of 'Pruden's Purple' tomato and I was thrilled to start my first purple heirloom.

That was also the summer I realized that our Australian cattle dog, Pearl, was a true garden dog. I'd moved to the Youngstown *Vindicator* that year. The people were relocating to California and had a couple of dogs they were trying to find homes for – and Pearl was one of them.

Pearl was like no other dog I'd ever seen. She was blue merle and she lay quietly at the feet of her owner. When I showed up to take her to her new home, she shook in the passenger seat of my truck the entire hour-long trip. When she got out, the truck was covered in her hair, something I would get used to over

Our tomato-loving dog Pearl stands above the garden – probably hoping to get to one of my ripe heirlooms before I do.

the next 15 years. And as she jumped down out of the truck she ran away – another thing I would get used to.

I chased her around the neighborhood for twenty minutes, finally catching the dog and walking her back home, holding her by the collar. She never would come when called and whenever there was an opportunity she would bolt, running full speed away from the house. She gladly walked right up to strangers; they would call us on the phone and I'd go get her.

That summer, I had just picked some kale and was talking to my wife Cindy, when I felt and heard this crunching. I looked down to see Pearl nibbling on the kale stalks as they dripped clear kale juice out of the ends. Now that's a garden dog.

As the season progressed, my first purple tomato started to turn and I was overjoyed to watch it turn from pink to purple. I figured it would be ready to pick in just a couple of days.

Pearl escaped that morning. Looking out my bathroom window I happened to see her wandering around in the backyard on her way to my tomato plant. I gasped as she started to pull the tomato off the vine, grabbing it with her mouth.

Off she went across the street, while I sprinted out the back door after her. Boy, she was fast. I finally caught her and rescued half of my tomato. After composing myself and getting my blood pressure back to normal, I actually saw the humor in the situation and decided to write a column about it for *The Vindicator*.

Later in the week, I was shooting photos in a courtroom. I'd worked in there a lot and gotten to know the judge and the bailiff pretty well. During a break in the trial, the judge looked down at me from the bench and said, "You ate the other half of that tomato, didn't you?"

"Your honor, I'm standing in court, I can't a lie: Yes, I ate the tomato."

The judge and bailiff couldn't stifle their laughter and neither could I.

Pearl passed away a few years ago, but I'll always remember her as the young dog who kept me running and who loved veggies from the garden as much as I do.

19

Pruning: How, When…and Why Bother?

Take me as I am…
— The Shirelles, "Will You Still Love Me," 1960

To prune or not to prune – what's the right thing to do? In my garden I never prune tomatoes. I'm too lazy and busy to be bothered, and I get plenty of tomatoes anyway. But other gardeners swear by it.

Old timers will tell you, pinch off the suckers to get better production. The theory is that by thinning the plant, all the energy will go into the main stem, possibly reducing the number of fruit, but giving you bigger tomatoes.

Suckers are those side shoots that grow in the crotch between the stem and the branch. Eventually they will become another main stem with branches, flowers and tomatoes of its own. The cycle continues with more suckers, and on and on.

My case for leaving the suckers alone is that they do have an important function: to shade the fruit. Tomatoes can get sun scald if foliage is sparse.

I love to leave my plants big and bushy, and since I mostly use cages that give good support, that works well for me. That being said, a tomato that's thinned might be less prone to fungal diseases, something I'm plagued with for a variety of reasons.

Another argument for pruning is that if you're relying on staking, the plants can become too much to handle for the stake. They can become cumbersome when not pruned.

The Two Main Growth Habits of Tomato Plants

This is a good time to talk about the difference between determinate and indeterminate tomatoes – because each group of plants has a different pattern of growth and production. Knowing which group your plants belong to will help you to think about their pruning needs.

Indeterminate Tomatoes – Most of the tomatoes I grow belong to this category. They will keep growing, producing tomatoes all season. Sometimes that means that their vines will grow eight feet or even longer (hence, the "indeterminate" label).

Pruning these will give you a compact plant with big tomatoes, but not as many as letting the vines go wild, like I do.

Some gardeners like to prune out everything below the first flower cluster, to develop a strong leader or center stem. Others will leave a couple of suckers on the lower portion of the plant, because they can be supported easily on stakes. The rest of the plant can be thinned by removing the suckers all the way to the top of the plant. But be warned: It's a weekly job, as the plants soar in the summer heat.

Determinate Tomatoes – These plants reach a certain height and stop growing, producing most of their tomatoes around the same time. Some types of determinate plants are bush, container or patio tomatoes. These varieties don't need any pruning; just let them grow to fruition.

The only other pruning that I recommend is at the end of the season. When the last frost date is about a month away, the plant can be topped to force what's left of the fruit to mature, or at least to begin to turn.

The Jury's Still Out on Pruning

Down at Janoski's Farm and Greenhouse in Clinton, Pa., they grow thousands of tomatoes, and for the last fifty years they've always pruned their tomatoes. But even though this has been a traditional task for them over the decades, they are now looking at leaving a few rows without pruning, to see how the plants do.

They're testing the theory that early pruning might damage the stem and possibly allow diseases or insects to get a hold on the plant.

What they are doing out on that farm is a good lesson for us as gardeners. Pruning suckers is a personal preference and depends on how you support your tomatoes. Like so many things in gardening it's about experimenting and figuring out what works for you.

Two tomato seedlings pop their heads up from the soil in my home greenhouse.

20

Harvesting, Sharing and Preserving

*It is apparent that no lifetime is long enough in which to
explore the resources of a few square yards of ground.*
— Alice M. Coats

When late summer arrives and all those tomatoes ripen – more than you can possibly eat – what's a gardener to do? An old joke has a bag of tomatoes being lobbed into the back seat of any car that pauses too long at the stop sign in front of the gardener's house.

But one of the real joys of gardening is giving away all those luscious tomatoes to friends, family, co-workers and the needy. Sure, all the people at work scoff at us gardeners, often pointing out how cheaply they can buy tomatoes in the store.

Those scoffers are the first ones in line when I bring in that ripe fruit, because they know deep in their heart there's nothing better. Almost everyone appreciates great, homegrown tomatoes and there is true joy in giving.

The food bank would love your extra tomatoes too. You might be surprised at who you are helping. Many of the recipients are the working poor, single mothers and seniors. They need fresh, nutritious produce just like everyone else. So if you've got some extra stuff from the garden, find a drop-off point at a church or other location so you can have the wonderful feeling of sharing.

Still have more tomatoes? Preserve 'em!

Ironically, with all the tomatoes I grow, I actually eat them all and never put up any. I could eat seven to ten tomatoes a day during the season and still long for more. But that's just me.

If you still have tomatoes left, and you probably will, there are several ways to preserve the harvest. Earlier, I talked about picking the tomatoes at the end of the season and saving them; but here are some other ideas.

Canning

Canning is an option that gardeners have used for as long as anyone can remember. Canning is an art that's been passed down for generations. It's something that I have never done, so I recommend learning from a seasoned pro.

It's easy enough to find a class on canning, and it's best to actually see someone complete the process and discuss the safety issues.

Freezing

If you're wary of canning, you might consider simply freezing your tomatoes to store them. The only drawback to this method is that it will change their texture.

For whole tomatoes it's pretty easy: Just wash and dry them, cut away the stem area, put them on a tray and freeze them. There's no need to blanch them to remove the skins; that can be done under warm water when they are thawed out.

Whether it's sauce, juice or some other recipe, frozen tomatoes retain the flavor well, but need the right application because of the loss of texture.

Keep those garden tomatoes for as long as possible. Anything to avoid those imposters that look, feel and sometimes taste like a tennis ball.

❧ SUN-DRIED TOMATOES ❧

These really keep their wonderful flavor and they are easy to make.

You can use a food dehydrator or the oven. There's variety of spices or salts you'll want to sprinkle on the tomatoes. I like a little sea salt and sometimes oregano.

I don't remove the skins or seeds from the tomatoes, though you might want to. Like most things gardening, it's about what works for you.

Using the Food Dehydrator

This is pretty foolproof. Lay some tomato slices on the rack so they are not touching, turn on the dehydrator, set around 140°F, and in a few hours the tomatoes will be done.

It takes a little practice to figure out when they are done. The tomatoes should be pliable, kind of leathery and still hold their color well.

Using the Oven

Preheat the oven to 150°F or the lowest setting you have. Mine will only go down to 170°F, but it still works. Set the tomatoes on a rack in the same manner as in the dehydrator and they will be done in around 12 hours, give or take a few hours. Check them every once in a while and you'll get the idea. It all depends on how thick the slices are and the temperature of the oven.

Storing and Rehydrating

They can be stored in plastic bags for a few weeks, or will last a year frozen. Some people like to vacuum seal the tomatoes and put them in the fridge or freezer. They'll last even longer.

They can be rehydrated by soaking them in water or other liquids or putting them right into a pot of sauce or soups. It usually takes a couple of hours for the rehydration process to be complete.

Tomato Bruschetta Starters

Bruschetta (pronounced bru-SKEH-ta, if you want to be very Italian about it. Your friends will correct you, but you'll be right) has become ubiquitous as a flavorful upgrade to bread and butter on the dining table. No wonder. It's a lovely way to showcase your favorite tomatoes, fresh garlic and basil.

What You Need:

6 to 8 of your favorite tomatoes,
  finally chopped
½ cup sun-dried tomatoes, finely chopped
  (Make your own for a real treat.
  See how on page 111.)
5 cloves fresh minced garlic
¼ cup olive oil

2 tablespoons balsamic vinegar
  (12-year-old is ideal)
½ cup fresh chopped basil
Sea salt and fresh ground pepper to taste
1 French baguette
2 cups fresh buffalo mozzarella cheese, sliced

Here's How:

Preheat the oven to the broiler setting.

In a large bowl, combine all the ingredients except the cheese and baguette and let sit for at least 10 minutes to release and blend all the flavors.

Cut the bread into ½ to ¾ inch slices, depending on how thick you like it. On a baking sheet lay out the bread in a single layer, broil for about a minute and don't take your eyes off it! Once it's lightly browned, the bread is ready.

Remove the baking sheet from the oven and spread the tomato mixture over the toasted bread. Then cover each piece with a little cheese. (You can leave the cheese off if you prefer a lighter dish, and serve just like this)

Broil for about 3 to 4 minutes, just until the cheese melts. Again, keep on eye on it while it's broiling. Burned mozzarella isn't fun. Serve immediately.

Serves 6.

21

The First and the Last: Extending the Tomato Season

Eating is an agricultural act.
— Wendell Berry

The race for the first tomato of the season might be the most important job in the summer garden, but sly gardeners know it's also necessary to plan for the last fruit of the season too.

Being the first to harvest a ripe fruit can be a neighborhood badge of honor, and it all starts with the right type of tomato.

There are certain varieties that have been bred for, or naturally produce, tomatoes in cool conditions – meaning you can get a jump on tomato season.

✕ THE FIRST ✕

A few years ago I ordered every early tomato I could find in the catalogs. Of all the exotic tomatoes I planted for my trial, the old reliable **'Early Girl'** took the prize for a medium-sized tomato that put on fruit early and also tasted good. It's been the standard for early tomatoes for decades and didn't disappoint when competing against all the others.

There were tomatoes that were ready sooner, but many were small cherries and others tasted bland.

The runners-up? **'Cosmonaut Volkov,' 'Whippersnapper,' 'Sungold,' 'Fourth of July'** and **'Juliet.'**

Now those winners really don't mean a thing; it's one man's opinion, and if the same trial were held again I'd bet there would be other winners.

With all things tomatoes, there are different opinions on how to get to harvest with the first one. I like to get seeds started early (months before the last frost of the season), grow the seedlings big and then put them in the garden when the soil is warm, sometimes with tiny green fruit already on the vine. Others say to plant early tomatoes six weeks before setting out and keep them growing strong from start to finish, planting them normally.

If you're not a seed starter, sometimes nurseries can provide plants early in the season for you to raise under lights.

Plants that you nurture will usually out-perform the small transplants provided by growers who have to take care of thousands. At least I like to think so.

Whichever way works best for you, one thing is for sure: The warmer the soil, the better the plants will do.

How to Warm up the Soil

There are lots of ways to get the soil temperatures up. I like to use black land-scape fabric, laid on the garden weeks before the tomatoes are planted outside. It lets water and air through, which is a good thing.

I tried black plastic one season, but felt that the soil was too dry at the end of the season. I later found out that commercial growers run drip irrigation under the plastic to keep the plants evenly moist.

Wall O' Water

In conjunction with the fabric, I have good luck using Wall O' Water plant protectors. They are really small, plant-sized greenhouses made of plastic. Their water-filled chambers surround a plant like an overcoat and keep it warm. During the day, the water absorbs heat and then releases it at night. One Wall O' Water goes around each plant.

But I like to put the Wall O' Water into the garden a week or two before planting, to heat the soil. Then when I plant out a small tomato transplant, I put the Wall O' Water back into place over the seedling until it actually pushes through the top of the plant protector.

In the right season that could mean tomatoes three or four weeks earlier than if you didn't give them that extra care.

A homemade version uses 2-liter clear plastic soda bottles filled with water and set up to surround a plant. Check online for other variations.

Close-up of 'Green Zebra', showing distinctive markings.

Red Plastic

Some growers have turned to a red plastic installed on the ground that reflects just the right spectrum of light and forces the plant to produce more tomatoes.

Tickling

Another trick to force the tomato to put fruit on early in the season is to tickle the flowers with an electric toothbrush. Tomatoes are self-pollinating, and need something like a bee to shake the flower so it will pollinate and put on tomatoes.

Early in the season bees may be few and far between, and the toothbrush will act like a bee and help pollinate the flower.

THE LAST: TOMATOES INTO WINTER

Although it's not as glamorous as the race for the first tomato of the season, feasting on garden tomatoes well into winter is a tradition that goes back hundreds of years.

Along with the tomatoes bred for early production, there are varieties that prefer to wait until the end of the season to ripen. Some, like **'Long Keeper,'** are not only excellent late tomatoes, they are also great storage tomatoes.

In my garden I head out as soon as we get a hard frost warning and pick everything off the vines. I sort out the tomatoes in the field. I put 'Long Keeper' and other large, firm beefsteaks in one bag and all the other tomatoes in another bag. *Tip:* Use double-bagged paper grocery bags, then a plastic bag around both of those.

Into the bag with most of the tomatoes goes an apple. The fruit produces ethylene gas which helps the tomatoes ripen. Those are the ones we'll be eating first.

In the 'Long Keeper' bag, it's just tomatoes. No hurry. We're happy if they keep us waiting well into the cool months.

All are stored in a cool area that doesn't freeze. I check the bags every week to see what's ready. A few tomatoes will rot, and some of the green ones won't turn, but what's harvested will put store-bought tomatoes to shame.

Extending the season will give you more tomatoes for a longer time, and that's all any grower could hope for as they enjoy juicy tomatoes before and after most of their neighbors.

Tomato Aioli

This wonderful recipe comes from my friend Chris Jackson, a talented chef in New York City who runs Ted & Honey Café Market in Brooklyn with his sister Michelle. Chris used to run a restaurant in Pittsburgh and we've known each other for years.

Folks who think aioli is just gussied up mayonnaise are missing out. Aiolis come in all sorts of flavors and can jazz up a simple menu. Serve this one with anything from a BLT with summer tomatoes, lettuces and crisp bacon, to grilled or smoked pork chops off the grill. You can even roll corn on the cob in it, then roll again in finely grated parmesan cheese, chili powder and lime juice!

What You Need:

2 Roma tomatoes or fresh garden tomatoes
1 cup light or blended olive oil
2 tablespoons tomato paste
3 egg yolks
4 tablespoons sun-dried tomatoes
2 tablespoons lemon juice
3 tablespoons chopped parsley
2 tablespoons roasted garlic cloves
   (or 1 tablespoon chopped fresh garlic)

2 tablespoons honey
1 tablespoon whole grain mustard
   (Dijon is fine)
1 tablespoon dry mustard
Salt and fresh cracked pepper to taste
Optional: add 4 tablespoons basil
   for stronger flavor

Here's How:

Cut fresh tomatoes in half, place on baking sheet cut side up and drizzle with olive oil, salt and pepper. Roast in a 350°F oven for half an hour to release all the flavors.

Let tomatoes cool for a few minutes, and then place the remaining ingredients except the oil into a food processor or blender and start the motor on high. As soon as everything seems blended, lower the speed and slowly add the remaining oil through the feeding shoot. Keep blending until ingredients emulsify – meaning it will all form into a thick yet silky aioli/mayonnaise consistency. Stop motor and taste. Add more seasoning if you like.

Makes 2 cups.

Shrimp Sandwich with Tomato Basil Aioli

Here's a convenient example of how Chris uses aioli to spice up a very simple dish.

What You Need:

10 jumbo cooked shrimp,
   tails removed, shrimp chopped
Good Italian bread cut into sandwich slices

¼ cup tomato basil aioli
   (use recipe preceding with basil variation)
½ cup of watercress and/or watercress sprouts

Here's How:

Take the shrimp and mix it with the aioli, thoroughly coating it, or simply spread the bread with the aoli, whatever your preference is.

The bread can be also spread with the aioli. Cover the shrimp with cress and make it into a wonderful sandwich.

22

GROWING TOMATOES IN COLD CLIMATES
(WITH A WORD ABOUT HOT CLIMATES, TOO)

*While the earth remaineth, seedtime and harvest, and cold and heat,
and summer and winter, and day and night shall not cease.*
— GENESIS 8:22

Growing tomatoes in colder climates can be challenging, but if there's one thing I've learned over the years, people will figure out a way to get their fresh, ripe tomatoes. If your winters are cold and you have your heart set on growing your own, you just need to know a few basic tricks, because without nice red fruit, there just isn't a garden.

The Right Site

In cool climates it's essential to select a good growing site. The perfect spot is a slight hillside facing the south, so you can take advantage of what sunlight you have. The sun will warm the soil; the rest is up to you. Just be sure to follow the suggestions in Chapters 6 and 7 about improving the soil, because growing in fertile, well-drained soil is essential to getting good quality tomatoes, no matter what your climate happens to be.

At the end of winter, anything you can do to get that garden bed as warm as possible as soon as possible is to the good.

✄ WARMING UP THE SOIL ✄

Black Landscape Fabric

As I described earlier, black landscape fabric or black plastic can be laid down on the bed to start warming the soil. Just be aware of the problem of leaving your soil too dry if you use the black plastic.

Mini Compost Piles

Another old trick to warm up the soil is to build a mini compost pile six or eight inches under the eventual bottom level of the planting hole. Use kitchen scraps and shredded leaves 50/50 – and maybe some well-aged manure – and mix them together. The scraps should be shredded or as small as possible. The process of composting will create heat, and then by the time summer rolls around, the added benefit of nutrients below the soil will feed the plants.

Protecting Your Early-Season Plants

There are two techniques I recommend for keeping your young plants warm until Mother Nature takes over: the Wall O' Water, which I talked about in the previous chapter; and something called a *cloche*.

Using a Cloche

A cloche is a miniature greenhouse placed over a plant or sometimes even an entire row. This is a technique that will extend your tomato season on both ends. Cloches were originally round glass bell jars placed over young plants to protect them from the cold (the word is French for "bell"). But a cloche can be made out of glass, plastic, floating row cover – anything transparent or translucent. A milk carton with the bottom cut out is a good example for plants when they are small. In zone 5 where I live, I've been to Janoski's Farm and Greenhouse in Clinton, Pa., in April, and seen them using hoops covered with two layers of floating row covers to get the earliest tomatoes.

If you take these steps to warm the soil, you'll be picking tomatoes in just about any climate.

✖ CHOOSING THE RIGHT TOMATO ✖

For the best results you'll want to choose the right tomato, one bred to produce tomatoes early. No matter what climate tomatoes are grown in, gardeners want them as soon as possible. Breeders are constantly working on creating tomatoes that taste good and set quickly.

'**Early Girl**' is one of my favorites. It produces tasty four to six ounce round red tomatoes. Although it wasn't the first tomato in a test of many early tomatoes, it was the best tasting.

'**Fourth of July**' is another hybrid I love. Four ounce tomatoes in trusses of six or so come quickly, 49 days after transplant, and continue all season. This is a very productive variety.

'**Siletz**' puts on bigger tomatoes, 10 to 12 ounces and is ready in a little over 60 days. This one has a thin skin and sweet acidic taste. It bears well and sets in clusters of three or four.

'**Sungold**' is an early sweet orange cherry that I talk a lot about. A favorite tomato for any climate.

'**Stupice**' is ready a little over 50 days from transplant. Its four ounce tomatoes are round and irregular shaped, and it's prolific and tasty.

'**Cosmonaut Volkov**' is an interesting hybrid from the Ukraine, named for a famous Russian cosmonaut who crashed while landing. It's not the first tomato of the season, taking a little over 70 days to ripen, but it's a winner – a medium-sized round red tomato prized for its taste.

'**Oregon Spring**' is one of many in a series of early tomatoes developed at Oregon State University. For some growers, this is one of the earliest tomatoes picked. It grows five ounce tomatoes that are round and red. Some say it's a little sweeter than 'Early Girl.'

❧ EARLY TOMATOES IN CONTAINERS ❧

Another way to get tomatoes to produce early is to grow them in containers. The pots need to be big able to hold at least five gallons of soil. To get them warm fast, set them up off the ground; a wood pallet or some bricks would work.

Keep them in full sun. If you have a stone patio, that's the place for the pots, because it will help keep the heat going and will take advantage of the reflective nature of stone.

❧ PROTECTING YOUR PLANTS FROM THE COLD ❧

Floating Row Cover

Early in the season your plants can be protected from cool spring winds by surrounding them with a floating row cover – or even plastic, as long as there is some kind of venting, so the plant doesn't get cooked on sunny days.

Cold Frame

A cold frame can give your tomatoes a jump start on the season. A cold frame is a transparent enclosure, like a greenhouse only usually with just one side made of clear material. I built one out of a picture window left out for the trash. This thing weighed about 70 pounds, but it was free and sitting on a curb. I'm sure it was quite a sight as I wrestled it into the back of my truck.

Whatever you use, glass, plastic or plexiglass, it should face south and be set at a 35-degree angle towards the sun. The clear window is attached to a frame with hinges so it can be opened and closed depending on the temperatures.

In my case, that window was way too heavy to open and close easily, a lesson learned. Keep that in mind when choosing something transparent to capitalize on the sun's energy.

If you could make a cold frame tall enough, the plants could grow in there for months until they had blossoms – or even tomatoes – by the time you put them in the garden.

Greenhouse

There are many different types, from free standing glasshouses for thousands of dollars to wood framed plastic structures for a few hundred.

I was blessed with an old Everlite greenhouse attached to the house I bought when I came to Pittsburgh in 1998. The Everlite was probably built in the 70's. Now, there's no way I could afford to heat it (I can barely afford to heat the house, built in 1939).

But even without heat, I can get my tomatoes into the garden early. In my zone 5 garden, I'll pick some 'Early Girl' and 'Sungold' tomatoes in June. The greenhouse works for so many other plants too. Cold weather crops can be in there almost all winter.

If you're absolutely determined to pick tomatoes early in a cool climate, I suggest you start early with seeds under fluorescent lights. Follow the instructions in the next chapter for basic seed starting.

Starting early does offer a new set of problems. Plants tend to get leggy, even under fluorescent lights. I've started plants early and sometimes laid them horizontally if they get too big. But an older tomato plant will only put tomatoes on during a certain timeline.

Some gardeners will start tomatoes six weeks before the last killing frost and use all the techniques above to get early tomatoes. If you're the type who enjoys experimenting, you could start a couple of plants even earlier and see which varieties will put on early tomatoes and keep churning them out for you all season long.

It's a baby now, but... Shot on an April day in my Ross Township greenhouse, this Burpee Experimental 2000 tomato was just starting out. I couldn't wait to see how big it would be by the end of May!

Horizontal Can Be a Good Idea

Earlier in the book I spoke about horizontal planting. It's especially relevant for early planting. It involves digging a shallow trench, turning the plant on its side, stripping off all but the top leaves and planting the seedling on its side. This keeps the roots close to the surface where things are warm and the plants will be happy.

⚘ GROWING TOMATOES IN HOT CLIMATES ⚘

Ironically, gardeners in hot climates can use plants that produce early tomatoes too. Many times the crop is grown in two seasons, the first starting in late winter until things get hot, and the second in late summer to early fall, and running until it gets cold.

In those warm climates it's important that the plant put on fruit before temperatures constantly hit 90 degrees. When this happens many plants won't set fruit.

Shade cloth can also help in the hottest areas. If temperatures are routinely over 90 degrees, the shade cloth can lower the heat by as much as 10 degrees.

Most of the cultural practices described in the book are extra-important in the heat, especially mulching and giving the plants enough water.

Whatever the climate, know that you're not alone in your quest for the longest possible growing season. Gardeners have worked for decades to ensure an extended harvest of fresh tomatoes.

Creamy Basil Roasted Garlic Tomato Soup

Wondering what else you can do with your end-of-the-season tomatoes? My wife Cindy and I sip on this soup on the last days that our sun porch is open, before the really cold weather sets in.

There are lots of variables to this recipe, mostly having to do with differences in texture. I enjoy a rustic style of soup with roughly chopped pieces; others might enjoy the soup with the ingredients run through a food processor. My recipes are a starting point, so go ahead and (re)make them yours.

What You Need:

2 heads roasted garlic, mashed
5 cloves garlic, minced
5 medium-sized tomatoes,
   blanched, peeled and diced
1 cup heavy cream

1 cup basil chiffonade
   (cut into long, thin strips)
Sea salt to taste
Fresh ground pepper to taste

Here's How:

Roast the garlic. If you have a garlic roaster, use that to bake the heads of garlic. If you don't have a roaster, you can put the garlic into a baking pan or even aluminum foil and prepare it like this: Preheat oven to 400°F. Put garlic heads in baking pan or roaster and drizzle with good olive oil. Cook for 30 to 45 minutes until brown. Remove garlic and let cool. Now peel the garlic and set the soft garlic aside to add to the soup later.

Core the tomatoes and blanch them by dipping them into a pan of boiling water for 15 seconds and letting them cool. The skins will slip off easily now.

Cut the tomatoes in half and remove the seeds by hand. I dice them at this point. If you want a finer texture, cut them into quarters and cook for 5 minutes in a saucepan with some olive oil. Then put them into a food processor

In a medium-sized saucepan heat up some olive oil and cook the minced garlic for a minute or so. Add the tomatoes and some salt and cook it all down for 10 minutes or so, until the consistency is right. If you want it thinner, add a little chicken stock; thicker, just keep it cooking.

Add the roasted garlic and heavy cream, season to taste with salt and pepper. Turn off the heat and add the basil. It will wilt in the soup but retain its wonderful flavor.

Serves 4.

Creamy Basil Roasted Garlic Tomato Soup
(see recipe on page 125)

23

A PASSION FOR SEEDS

"Don't judge each day by the harvest you reap
but by the seeds that you plant."
– ROBERT LOUIS STEVENSON

Drive down long rural roads at night anywhere in the country, and you'll see the glow of fluorescent lights from basement windows, exposing the presence of tomato growers bent on picking the first fruit in the neighborhood.

In late winter they walk downstairs and unpack their seeds, lovingly planting them with dreams of tall vines filled with perfect tomatoes.

What brings on such passion and devotion?

When we first start gardening, we're thrilled when something just makes it through the season: "It lived, hurray!" But after a while we long to grow something different from the usual, or a plant that we have fallen in love with, but can't find anywhere. That's what growing from seed is all about. It allows us to grow varieties that are not likely to be found at local nurseries.

About Those Lights

Lighting is key for seed starting, and fluorescent shop lights are a great, cheap way to provide it. You hang them from chains just inches above the plants and then move them up incrementally as the plants grow. Nothing to it. Some gardeners put them on a timer for 16-18 hours, but I let my lights run 24 hours a day.

Here's a trick I learned from other indoor growers: Drape aluminum foil over the lights, surrounding the plants with the reflective material. The foil will bounce the light around and the plants love it.

There are other types on indoor lighting specifically designed for growing plants that will work fine, but they're more expensive than the shop lights. If your intention is just to start the transplants and get them out into the garden, I'd go with the shop lights. They can also be used for growing lots of other plants, not only seedlings.

Do you have a large south-facing windowsill? That can work, too, depending on the amount of sunlight the season provides. But indoor lights are more reliable.

When to Start the Seeds

Now that the lighting is in place, it's time to decide when to start the seeds. That's the number one question for beginners. Planting is like comedy, it's all about timing. The idea is to have a plant that sprouts and grows continually, unchecked, until it's time to set it out in the garden.

Starting seeds six to eight weeks before the planting date is perfect. But if it's your first year planting, you might not be able to wait for the calendar to tell you when – I know I couldn't. I started some plants months early just to see what happened. I ended up with a three-foot-long tomato plant lying prostrate under one of the lights. With the help of my kids we carefully moved the plant out into the garden and planted it, using a technique called trenching (page 98), which gives long, leggy tomatoes like that one a chance to thrive. That plant did great, by the way, so there's more than one way to start tomatoes.

Preparing the Containers and Planting the Seeds

Finding a good seed-starting mix is the first step. Forget potting soil or garden dirt; instead, use a fine, light mix specifically made to start and grow seeds in.

One trick that gardeners learn eventually (took me a few years) is to moisten the soil first before putting it into whatever containers you're going to use. Don't do what I did when I first started gardening indoors, which was to put the dry mix into the container, add the water and watch as the mix flies out everywhere.

The mix should be moist but not dripping wet; it takes time to figure out the right texture: Better to be too dry than too wet. Water can always be added. If it's too wet add more dry mix.

I start my seeds in the old six-packs from last year's annuals. They're perfect. If you didn't save them, they can be purchased at a good garden center. But almost anything with drainage will work.

Once your containers are filled, gently drop in the seeds, then lightly cover with more moist mix. Pat the mix down to assure good contact between the soil and the seed. For good germination, temperatures should stay around 65°F to 75°F.

What about egg cartons? I often talk to gardeners who want to use egg cartons, and I advise against it. Because of their size, they need to be watered too often, sometimes once a day, depending on the size of the plant.

Tending the Sprouts

Now put the containers under the lights and cover them with clear plastic to retain the moisture. Remove the plastic as soon as the seeds sprout, in about a week. If you leave the covering on after that, it can cause all sorts of problems, like damping off – which is when the seeds sprout and rot at the stem. This will put you a week behind in planting.

TIP: *An oscillating fan on a timer running for a couple of hours a day will simulate outdoor conditions and make the plants stronger.*

Keep the lights an inch from the top of the plants as they grow. When they put on their first true leaves (right after the first foliage) it's time to start once-a-week fertilizing.

Begin at half strength, and over the next few weeks increase the dilution to full strength – until a week before the plants are going out.

Seedling close-up. This little tomato seedling clings to the seed before shedding the seed coat.

Hardening Off: Getting Your Babies Used to the Big World

Tomatoes that are growing under lights can't go right out into the garden without a period of adjustment called *hardening off*. For a couple of days before the plants are set outside, slow down the watering and fertilizing.

Then, on the first day of hardening off, put them outside in a protected spot for a couple of hours, the second day a little longer and so forth – until after seven days they have been outside all day.

Now, that's the way you're supposed to do it. But truth be told, I rarely harden my plants off and they struggle for a week or so and still do fine. I've just got too many plants to even think about moving them in and out for a week.

Besides, I'm busy writing books, producing radio shows and occasionally seeing my family.

Actually, since my plants go from my basement directly into a greenhouse and grow in full sun with the protection of a pane of glass, they fare a little better than plants that lived under lights.

If you can't get them hardened off before planting out, just cover the small transplants with some protection, like a floating row cover, after putting them in the ground. It's a wonderful garden tool that has many purposes: The spun bound translucent fabric is so lightweight the plants themselves hold it up. It will also be a good sun block for the plants, as they are susceptible to sunburn early on.

Now your plants are ready to be planted in amended soil filled with nutrients that will keep them happy all summer.

For me, time in a basement bathed in fluorescent light and filled with the scent of tomatoes is a prelude to longer days and dreams of walking barefoot in the garden alongside eight-foot-tall dark green plants covered in a rainbow of colored tomatoes.

24

'COMPOST SURPRISE'

Despite the gardener's best intentions, Nature will improvise.
— MICHAEL P. GAROFALO, GARDEN WRITER, POET

Surprises in the garden make our world go around.

Early on, after a few years of gardening, I had a compost pile to be proud of. Each spring the top of the pile would offer up volunteers from not-yet-decomposed seeds. Potatoes, cucumbers, pumpkins, tomatoes or something else would pop out, offering me something to watch and examine throughout the season.

Yes, it was always a risk, those mystery seedlings, but one worth taking; the anticipation was akin to a kid at Christmas.

I'd guess it was the third or fourth year I was gardening that I spotted a particularly vigorous tomato plant emerging from the compost pile. I named it 'Compost Surprise' and watched in amazement as it grew by leaps and bounds over the summer, putting on long trusses of ping pong ball-sized red fruit.

When the tomatoes closest to the stem turned deep red I picked a couple and popped them into my mouth. I can still remember the zing they had, a high acid tomato that was the perfect match for my taste buds. 'Compost Surprise' was a juicy tomato that would explode with flavor. Bigger than a cherry, but smaller than a sauce tomato, it was the perfect size to snack on in the garden. As a warm tomato right off the vine, it excelled.

The trusses kept coming and the plant filled with colorful fruit. Eventually, I couldn't keep up with them outside and had to share my secret with the rest of the family. They loved the tomato – that trademark zing was really something else. I hoped for a winner that I could save seed from for years to come.

The following year I planted the seeds I'd saved from 'Compost Surprise,' but what I got didn't resemble Surprise at all: It was a misshapen, bland tasting beefsteak. The ultimate disappointment. Christmas never came for 'Compost Surprise.'

How do I explain what happened? The original tomato that sprouted for me was probably from a hybrid, which meant that its seeds wouldn't grow true and would never be a duplicate of 'Compost Surprise.'

It's been over 15 years now, and I'm still searching for a tomato that even comes close. I know it's out there; the chase is half the fun.

Mango Ketchup

Here's another great Chris Jackson recipe. This updated classic works well with tomatoes from a can, or even better, last season's jarred tomatoes! To really give it extra zing, try fresh tomatoes from the garden, in their own juices.

What You Need:

1 28 oz. can whole, crushed plum tomatoes
   (see below for fresh tomato option)
1 28 oz. can tomato puree
   (omit if you are using fresh tomatoes)
$^1/_8$ cup olive oil
2 medium sweet onions, diced

$^1/_8$ cup tomato paste
1½ cups dark brown sugar
1 cup cider vinegar
1 cup frozen mango puree, or
   2 fresh mangoes peeled and pureed
1 tablespoon kosher salt, plus a little extra to taste

Here's How:

Heat olive oil in heavy-bottomed 6-quart saucepan over medium-high heat. When oil is hot add diced onions and cook until lightly browned and caramelized.

Add tomato paste and cook for an additional 2 minutes (this gets some of the acidity out).

Add the rest of the ingredients with a tablespoon of salt and bring to a simmer until reduced slightly and thickened to a ketchup-like consistency.

Pull from heat and puree with a stick blender or tabletop blender in batches.

Taste and check for seasoning, then pour into container of choice and refrigerate for up to a month.

Fresh Tomato Option: You will need 7 to 8 cups of tomatoes (measured after they've been sliced or diced). First, score an X into the bottom of each with a paring knife. Then plunge in boiling water for 15 to 30 seconds and then immediately plunge into ice water to cool. Peel tomatoes and then crush them by hand in a bowl, reserving the juices. Use in place of canned tomatoes and tomato puree.

Serves 4 to 6.

25

SAVING SEEDS

*"Though I do not believe that a plant will spring up where
no seed has been, I have great faith in a seed. Convince me that you
have a seed there, and I am prepared to expect wonders."*
— HENRY DAVID THOREAU

For centuries, gardeners carefully saved seeds from their prized tomatoes and passed them along to the next generation.

These days it's easier to just order a few packets, but saving seeds will also save you a little money, and it's a fun project that can involve the whole family. Best of all, you could be creating a variety that's tailor-made to your own taste... and to your own microclimate.

Which Seeds to Save

First, determine if the plant in question is open pollinated or a hybrid.

Open pollinated (non-hybrid)

These plants have developed the "natural" way, usually without human intervention. (Though some were created by crosses, they are not called hybrids.) Their seeds will give you a plant that is exactly like its parent plant.

Hybrid

These plants are the result of crossing different varieties and selecting for certain traits. When hybrid seed is saved, the next season it will not grow true, meaning it will look like one of its parents, but not be an exact copy of what grew last season. It can also produce some interesting results. Hybrid seed, though, has a low germination rate and can even be sterile. Hybrids are always labeled as such on the seed packet or nursery tag.

Four Simple Steps

1. Whether your plants are hybrid or open pollinated, try to save seed from the first fruits, selecting for the trait of earliness (a very desirable trait in tomatoes). Allow the fruit to over-ripen a little but not rot. This will provide mature seed.

   TIP: *In all plants it's important to save seeds that are fully developed. They will produce the best plants for you.*

2. Tomato seeds need to be fermented. Cut the tomato in half and squeeze out the seed into a glass of water. Stir the contents once a day for three days. The fermentation process removes the gelatinous coating around the seed that nature put there to prevent it from sprouting inside the tomato. Fermentation also kills certain diseases that can affect the fruit.

3. Dry the seed. I find a coffee filter works well because the seed doesn't stick to it the way it would to a paper towel.

4. After a couple of days, label and put the seed in an airtight container and store it in a cool, dry place. Canning jars are a good choice. Some growers put silica gel in the jar to assure that the seeds stay dry.

Seeds are living, breathing organisms. You can extend the life of seeds by slowing down their respiration in cool, dry conditions, Properly stored seed can last for years, even decades. The other day while getting ready to sow a fall crop of lettuce, I stumbled onto a packet of 'Oxheart' tomato seeds from a decade ago. It was an old heirloom favorite that I had forgotten about. When I planted them, just about every seed sprouted.

I remember the first year I saved seeds and planted them the next season. I was pleasantly surprised at germination rates that exceeded 90 percent. You can bet I basked in the glory of my flats of tomato seedlings.

As Time Goes By...

Seeds saved from your garden should evolve over the years by reacting and changing to the climate of your garden. Experienced savers look for different traits from different plants to perpetuate. While earliness is prized in tomatoes, there are also other things to consider, like disease resistance, vigor and of course, taste. It's yours to pursue and yours to enjoy.

Maybe someday you'll be passing along a mason jar filled with favorites to your own children.

Tomato Basil Salad

Donato Coluccio practices what he preaches – he's a big believer in the less-is-more approach when it comes to fresh tomatoes. This is one of his classics.

What You Need

2 fresh, ripe tomatoes,
2 oz. buffalo mozzarella sliced ¼-inch thick
2 teaspoons fresh basil chiffonade
  (cut into long, thin strips)
2 tablespoons extra virgin olive oil

1 teaspoon balsamic vinegar
  (Chef Coluccio recommends 12-year-old
  balsamic for the best flavor)
Fresh cracked pepper to taste
Sea salt to taste

Here's How:

Slice 1 tomato into ½ to ¾-inch thick slices. Lay slices on a plate. Dice the other tomato.

On top of the sliced tomatoes, layer mozzarella, diced tomatoes, basil, salt and pepper.

Drizzle vinegar, then olive oil over the dish.

Serves 1 or 2.

26

TOMATO PESTS

The garden suggests there might be a place where we can meet nature halfway.
— MICHAEL POLLAN

There are many pests that are attracted to tomatoes, but few that can really destroy the crop. My advice is to do everything you can in the garden to invite beneficial insects into the environment. Those beneficials will do a great job for you. One of the greatest benefits to gardening organically is letting nature do the work. There are other organic methods of control, as well, and I'm going to tell you about which work best with the various kinds of pests.

Here's a who's who of tomato pests – the damage they do, how to spot them and what you can do about them:

✄ WHAT'S EATING YOUR TOMATOES? ✄

Whitefly

One of the most visible pests is the whitefly when mature. They're very easy to identify: When you shake the branches, a cloud of white insects will fly off the plant. In my garden they are most prevalent at the end of the season; in that case I don't do anything about them.

They reproduce quickly – they're the rabbits of insect pests. They start as a crawling insect, then molt into a flattened stationary greenish insect that sticks to the leaves. Eventually we see the flying mature insect. They can have a few generations each season depending on your climate. Females lay up to about 100 eggs at a time on the underside of leaves.

They have piercing mouthparts for sucking; the damage is similar to aphids. On tomato plants they cause deformed new growth and wilting, but worse than that, the insect can spread diseases.

> **CONTROL TIPS:** *Spray insecticidal soap, horticultural oil or Neem (I only use Neem as a last resort though, because if used incorrectly it could harm bees and other beneficials). Be sure to coat the undersides of the leaves wherever you see the pest. It usually takes two or three applications over a month to get them under control.*

Since whiteflies thrive in a greenhouse environment, one of the most important controls is to examine plants before you bring them home from the nursery, to ensure that they are not infected with the pest.

Aphids

Aphids are similar to whiteflies in their damage; they suck sap from the plant. They are soft-bodied, pear-shaped, tiny insects often found on the undersides of leaves. They can be a host of colors, green, yellow or brown. They excrete honeydew which turns into sooty mold. And that sweet treat attracts ants. The presence of ants on your tomato plants is often the first tip that you've got an aphid problem.

The beneficial insect that helps to control aphids is the **ladybug**. Aphids are the favorite meal for ladybug larvae.

> **CONTROL TIPS:** *If the infestation is minimal, blast the little suckers off the plants with a strong stream of water. Going one step further, insecticidal soap, horticultural oil and Neem are all effective tools to keep aphids under control.*

Spider Mites

Spider mites are very small and often can't be identified just by sight. They leave a telltale webbing; that's the clue that they have invaded the tomato patch. Following severe infestations, leaves become discolored, turning gray.

Organic gardeners stand a better chance in dealing with them, since chemical pesticides kill most of the spider mite's predators, which ultimately allows them to reproduce at will – negating the purpose of using the chemicals in the first place.

> **CONTROL TIPS:** *The best controls are the same as for whitefly and aphid: Spraying with insecticidal soap, horticultural oil or Neem.*

Tomato Hornworm

The tomato hornworm can be impossible to spot, even though it's a caterpillar and thick as a thumb and four inches long. Some people call them ugly, but the 12-year-old inside me finds them beautiful.

The adult moth, which lays the eggs on both sides of the leaves, is sometimes called the sphinx, hawk, or hummingbird moth. The latter is what I've always called it and when I see one around, I know that somewhere down the line I'll find a hornworm. The moth is a mottled gray-brown color with yellow spots on the sides of the abdomen, and a wingspread of about five inches. It emulates a hummingbird in the way it flies and feeds.

I usually discover them on a trip out to the garden when I'll be dumbstruck by

When a tomato hornworm has these rice-like eggs on its back, don't kill it. The worm has already stopped feeding on your plant because those eggs belong to a parasitic wasp, and they will hatch out and eat the worm from the inside. By not killing the worm you're perpetuating the life cycle of this non-stinging beneficial insect – one of the good guys in your tomato patch.

discovering a whole branch of a tomato plant chewed away. "What the hell…" I say, every time. Then my brain reacts and I think "Ahh, hornworm of course." I follow the damage around the plant, even sometimes noticing a tomato half-eaten.

It takes a good eye to find them because their defense is coloring that blends in with the foliage. The worms are green with white and black markings and on their forehead is a scary-looking horn.

Last season I tracked one on a plant, and when I finally found it, I didn't need to remove it. Why? The worm was covered in rice-like egg sacks from a **parasitic wasp,** a very beneficial insect. This indicated to me that the hornworm had stopped feeding on my tomato plant and was dying. The wasp larvae had emerged from the eggs and eaten their host up from the inside. They'd soon be releasing another generation of wasps with their bellies full of hornworm.

Leaving the wasp larvae to do their work instead of removing the worm perpetuates the natural cycle of life, and that's something the garden needs.

If you see one that's not infected with the wasp eggs, just remove the worm and kill it. Usually, I'll only find one or two per season.

When my kids were younger I would put the caterpillar in a ventilated jar with lots of tomato foliage and send it into school at the start of the year. That was always a hit.

Stink Bugs

Stink bugs are green or brown, and shaped like a shield. They smell bad when crushed (hence their name). The insect pierces buds and tomatoes, causing the buds to drop and fruit to be deformed. They secrete a toxic substance from their salivary glands which kills the cells surrounding the feeding sites.

CONTROL TIPS: *Fall cleanup is important since the stink bug overwinters in garden debris. Horticultural oil and Neem are good choices to control these bugs.*

Flea Beetles

Flea beetles are a common pest of tomatoes, especially in the seedling stage. They are tiny and make perfectly round holes in foliage. This pest drives gardeners crazy because they are rarely seen. They jump like fleas from plant to plant. Their damage is rarely serious, just annoying. Cool mornings are a good time to go out with a hand-held vacuum to suck up the beetles.

> **CONTROL TIPS:** *Crop rotation and good cultural practices at the end of the season are a good start for flea beetles. A thick layer of mulch inhibits the larvae from emerging from beneath the plants. Spinosad, horticultural oil and Neem are effective treatments for flea beetles.*

Cabbage Loopers

The cabbage looper is best known as the green worm that does a number on cole crops (cabbage, kale, broccoli and the like), but it also can be found munching on tomato leaves.

The cabbage looper moth is the white one we see hovering in the garden; it lays eggs that hatch out to become the cabbage looper. The pest can have a couple of generations a season. I can remember as a kid trying to catch them on cool mornings without success. The worm itself is about an inch long and luminescent green. It's well camouflaged against the foliage of the cole crops (except red cabbage). They are most often discovered by searching for their frass (excrement).

For cole crops we just cover them with a floating row cover at planting time. For tomatoes, that would work for only a short time, because they grow so fast and need help with pollination – so the cover is not practical.

> **CONTROL TIPS:** *Inspect the plants, especially the undersides of leaves, and destroy bunches of yellow eggs. Bacillus thuringiensis (or Bt, as it's better known) is a good organic control for the worm.*

Cutworms

Cutworms can be a problem at planting time. There's nothing more heartbreaking than walking out into the garden one morning and seeing all your tomato and pepper plants lying prostrate on the soil.

The worms are one or two inches long and often curl into a ball when disturbed. They feed at night and hide in debris and soil at the base of plants.

To feed, the cutworm wraps itself around the base of the plant, and must make contact all the way around, to allow it to eat.

> **CONTROL TIPS:** *The best way to beat them is to install some type of barrier around the stem of the tomato. Even a toothpick on two sides of the stem will stop the cutworm. Some gardeners use empty cardboard toilet paper or paper towel rolls, slit down the middle and made into a cuff around the stem. Aluminum foil will work, and plastic pots and old tin cans – just something to stop the worm from circling around the stem.*

Colorado Potato Beetle

The Colorado potato beetle is a bigger problem on its namesake potato, but they've been known to attack tomatoes, too, since both plants are in the same family.

The adult is black and yellow striped, and the larva is black spotted. Both the adult and larva will feed on the foliage of tomatoes. An infestation can possibly kill a plant.

The beetles overwinter in the garden soil as adults. When things warm up they start feeding on whatever they can find. Look for their tiny, yellowish-orange eggs on the undersides of leaves and crush them.

> **CONTROL TIPS:** *Bacillius thuringiensis var. tenebrionis (Bt) works against small larvae. Spray with Bt as soon as the larvae are discovered. If you miss that window of opportunity spray the plants with Spinosad or Neem.*

Tomato Fruitworm

The tomato fruitworm has many names, depending on the crop it's attacking. They are also called corn earworm, cotton bollworm, soybean podworm, or sorghum headworm. One thing for sure: They can really put a dent in a crop of tomatoes. The moth lays eggs singly on younger leaves and around developing fruit. The eggs are round and white, then develop a reddish band right before they hatch. When that happens, the larvae burrow into the tomatoes near the cap, making them inedible (unless you have a good knife and a strong stomach.)

> **CONTROL TIPS:** *The worms can be handpicked. You can purchase beneficial nematodes to deal with them too, and Bt can be effective. The good news is that tomato fruitworms are a natural prey of parasitic wasps (see tomato hornworm, above).*

Tomato Budworms

Tomato budworms are similar to the fruitworms and are controlled the same way. They're more prevalent in the South, but can be found in the North, too.

I hope you aren't feeling overwhelmed by the thought of all these pests. It's unlikely that more than a few of them will ever descend on your tomato plants in any growing season. And now, if you want to garden organically, you have some tools to help you start working with nature, not against her. That will always give you better results, both short term and in the long run.

From my own experience in dealing with pests, one of the best things you can do is spend time in the garden just sitting and watching your plants. You'll see things that normally go unnoticed. When you see the leaf of a tomato plant move, slowly walk over and see what's going on. You might get a look at the epic battle between good bug and bad bug.

Get a magnifying glass and spend an hour one morning looking at the foliage of your plants. I'm betting you'll discover a whole new world, and if that discovery includes some of the bad guys, you'll know just what to do.

Quick Guide to Tomato Pests and Organic Controls

PEST	CONTROLS
Whitefly	Insecticidal soap, horticultural oil, Neem
Aphid	Insecticidal soap, horticultural oil, Neem
Spider Mite	Insecticidal soap, horticultural oil, Neem
Tomato Hornworm	Handpick, parasitic wasps
Stink Bugs	Fall cleanup, horticultural oil, Neem
Flea Beetles	Crop rotation, Spinosad, horticultural oil, Neem
Cabbage Looper	Bt
Cutworms	Cutworm collars
Colorado Potato Beetle	Bt
Tomato Fruitworm	Handpick, Bt, beneficial nematodes
Tomato Budworm	Handpick, Bt, beneficial nematodes

27

TOMATO DISEASES

When one of my plants die, I die a little inside, too.
— LINDA SOLEGATO

One of the things I do is co-host a radio garden show. Each spring, I hear caller after caller saying, "Help…the bottom leaves of my tomatoes are turning yellow and drying up!"

Welcome to the wonderful world of tomatoes. Regardless of what we do as gardeners, if there's a wet season you're likely to have fungal diseases.

Some gardeners spray their plants with organic fungicides or compost tea, but there are lots of other things you can do that will help. First, let's talk about the most common diseases and later I'll go into more depth about some cultural practices that can help.

✄ DISEASES ✄

Early Blight

Early blight is one of the most prevalent. It's what many of those callers are panicking over. It usually starts with concentric rings developing on older leaves, and then turning them yellow. I remove the leaves as they die. You need to be careful not to spread the disease from one plant to another by touching a healthy plant with anything used on an infected one. Using pruners? Dip them in a 10% bleach solution between cuts.

The good news: Plants will usually outgrow early blight; they'll lose leaves, but produce plenty of fruit.

Gray Leaf Spot

Gray leaf spot only affects the leaves, starting with the oldest. Look for small dark spots on both sides of the leaves. They'll get bigger and then turn grayish brown. After time, the centers of the spots will crack and fall out. The surrounding areas will turn yellow and the leaves will dry up and fall off.

Powdery Mildew

Powdery mildew is a common problem with many other plants besides tomatoes and usually won't kill the plant. It starts with white patches on the upper surface of leaves. Spots can develop into brown lesions, causing the leaves to drop off.

Something to do before you see powdery mildew: Spray your plants with a mixture of one tablespoon of baking soda and one teaspoon of dish soap in one gallon of water.

Fusarium Wilt (can be fatal)

Fusarium wilt attacks only certain tomato cultivars. Plants infected by this soil-borne fungus have yellow leaves that wilt starting at the bottom leaves. At first, only one side of the leaf will be affected, then the disease spreads to the rest of the plant. Plants will die early and often won't produce any fruit at all. Best prevention: Buy plants that are bred to be disease resistant (more on that below).

Late Blight

Late blight affects the leaves and tomatoes. It's actually the disease that caused the Irish Potato Famine. It starts with gray, greasy-looking spots on the leaves. Sometimes a ring of white mold can appear around those spots, especially when it's wet. The spots eventually turn dry and papery. Stems can turn black and the tomatoes can also develop greasy gray spots.

Septoria Leaf Spot

Septoria leaf spot looks a lot like late blight, but the papery patches on the leaves develop tiny, dark specks inside them. Older leaves, starting at the bottom of the plant, are affected first.

Southern Blight (can be fatal)

Southern blight has a white mold growing on the stem near the soil line. Dark, round spots will appear on the lower stem and both the outer and inner stem will become discolored. Southern blight fungus girdles the tomato stem and prevents the plant from taking up water and nutrients. Young plants may collapse at the soil line.

Tomato plant infected with a fungus. Fungal diseases can be a problem when the weather is cool and wet.

Verticillium Wilt

Verticillium wilt is a soil-borne fungus that can affect many different vegetables. Plants will wilt during the hottest part of the day, recovering in the evening. You'll see yellowing and then eventually, brown between the leaf veins, starting with the leaves at the bottom of the plant. The inside of the stems will be discolored too.

Anthracnose

Anthracnose is another common fungus problem causing tomatoes to rot. The fruit will have small, roundish, sunken spots. The spots progressively get bigger and darken in the center.

Bacterial Speck

Bacterial speck manifest as tiny, raised, dark spots, usually with a white border on the fruit.

Blossom End Rot

Blossom end rot appears at the bottom of the fruit with dark spots that get bigger as the fruit rots. See pages 33 and 100 for more discussion.

A healthy-appearing tomato plant. Few tomato diseases are fatal, but keep an eye out for changes in the leaves, fruit and stem.

Buckeye Rot

Buckeye rot is more common in the South, especially during wet weather. It's like blossom end rot, except occurring on green fruit instead of red. On ripened fruit, the rotting area will appear water-soaked, but not dark in color. The rot develops on the area of the fruit that touches the soil. The spot will enlarge and develop concentric rings that resemble a buckeye. The affected area is smooth, distinguishing it from late blight, which has a rough surface.

Gray Wall

Gray wall is a problem with ripening fruit. The green fruits have a gray cast or gray blotches. Ripe fruit will have green or brown areas on the inside of the fruit.

What To Do

Good cultural practices can help gardeners help fight off these tomato diseases. First, when possible, purchase disease-resistant varieties. How will you know? They will have a capital letter after the name of the plant (like V for resistance to verticillium wilt, F for fusarium wilt, and so on). When in doubt, ask your nurseryman.

Other actions you can take:

- Give your plants plenty of air circulation. They should be planted at least three feet apart. Some home gardeners space them five feet apart.

- Mulch, mulch and mulch some more. The mulch does wonders for tomatoes. It stops soil-borne fungal spores from splashing up onto the leaves. It also keeps the plant stay evenly moist. It's the best way to avoid blossom end rot.

- Rotate crops every season. When possible, the garden should be on a rotation plan so that the same crop isn't growing in the same spot year after year. Soil-borne diseases will attack the same type of plant if grown in the same spot every season, and the diseases will thrive there. In my case, though – and for anyone with a small space to work in – I only have one place to plant tomatoes with enough sun to make them thrive. What do I do? What can you do? Pile compost on the bed every year. It's a great deterrent.

- It's important to water in the morning when needed, and always at the base of the plant. This allows the foliage to dry out during the day, which will help beat fungal diseases. Tomatoes only need one inch of water a week. When rain doesn't provide that, soak the plants early in the day.

- Don't work with the plants when they are wet; this could pass the diseases from one plant to another.

- Be sure to clean up any plant debris during and at the end of the season. Diseases (and pests) will overwinter in the shriveled vines, leaves and fruit.

- Grow your plants in good soil filled with compost and other organic amendments. Plants that aren't struggling will fight off disease better than a plant barely making it.

- What about organic fungicides? They are an option, but I don't like to use them around food crops. One of the most effective for tomatoes is based on copper; I just don't like the idea of using it on something I eat.

  If you do use a fungicide, the trick is to apply it *before* you see signs of damage. When the weather is cool and wet, get your fungicide on.

- Succession planting will help with fungal diseases. Tomato plants that are put in the ground two weeks after the first crop seem to be able to fight off the diseases, maybe due to being planted in soil that's already nice and warm. When I planted those 'Sungold' tomatoes in mid-June they grew wonderfully with no signs of disease. However, most of my early planting succumbed to late blight, which is one of the saddest things that can happen to someone who enjoys picking those end of the season tomatoes and letting them ripen into early winter.

I really feel that, regardless of what you do, if the season is a cool and wet one, tomatoes will be affected by fungal diseases; but that doesn't mean you won't get tomatoes. Follow the tips above and cross your fingers. It's something we all do sometimes when dealing with Mother Nature.

28

BRAGGING

Pride goeth before a fall.
— PARAPHRASE OF PROVERBS 16:18

Bragging is one of my many faults, but we gardeners just can't help ourselves sometimes. There's always a competition between all of us to harvest the first tomato of the year. It's a big deal.

Now, my wife's favorite tomato happens to be 'Sungold,' an orange cherry that's sweet as sugar, as I've mentioned before. It's also an early tomato. One year I started a bunch in March that were ready to harvest in June – that's really early for tomatoes. But what good is having super-early tomatoes if no one knows you've got 'em, right?

At work I tried to steer the conversation towards tomatoes with some of my gardening buddies. "When do you guys think you're going to start picking tomatoes?" I asked innocently. They hemmed and hawed and mumbled something about July or August, then asked me what I wanted to hear: "When do you think you'll be picking *your* tomatoes, Doug?" I couldn't answer fast enough as I explained that the little golden fruit were just turning and it would be only a couple of days until we'd be eating fresh garden tomatoes. I wish I had a camera to capture the look on one of my friends as he said something I was used to hearing: "I hate you," not really meaning it.

That night we had a terrible thunderstorm and a huge black cherry tree fell across my white picket fence around the garden, crushing the three 'Sungold' plants that were ready for picking.

The next morning, after Cindy left for work, I went out to check on the storm damage and found the downed tree. Struck by the carnage Mother Nature had unleashed, I ran to get my chainsaw. You would have thought a baby was trapped under the tree as I frantically worked to free Cindy's tomato plants. The aroma of tomato foliage filled the air, mixed with the smell of oil.

Half an hour of cutting and I was finally able to see what was left. The plants were a total loss, crushed and mangled. Their tomato cages, on the other hand, still live on today, misshapen but functional.

What was I going to tell my wife? A crop failure for her 'Sungold' wasn't good news for an Italian cook who counted on them. Luckily, I had three more 'Sungold' plants on the patio that I hadn't set out yet. They looked sickly, though, since they had been there for a good month – leggy and drooping over the rims of their six-inch pots, touching the ground. I knew this was the only source for this tomato in June and also realized I had nothing to lose by planting them.

Well, these plants took off, loving the warm summer soil. By the end of the season they were still healthy and thriving, giving Cindy lots of her favorite tomatoes, while other plants I'd started in May were succumbing to fungal diseases after a particularly wet season.

I learned a couple of lessons that summer: Succession planting for tomatoes can save the day and, most importantly, keep your mouth shut and don't brag about the garden. One of those two lessons was taken to heart.

Smoked Tomato Pepper Jam

Here is my secret weapon for bringing out and complementing the flavor of pork chops and other meat-based menus. It's another Chris Jackson recipe and it can be prepared well ahead of time.

What You Need:
2 pounds fresh tomatoes Roma tomatoes
(or any thick-skinned tomato)
4 tablespoons extra virgin olive oil
2 Spanish onions, finely chopped
    (or any large, mild and sweet onion)
1 tablespoon chopped garlic
2 bell peppers, diced into small pieces
6 jalapeño peppers, diced fine,
    seeds removed
1 pinch red pepper flakes – optional
1 cup brown sugar
1 tablespoon ground cumin
1 tablespoon kosher salt, plus a little
    extra to taste
1 teaspoon fresh cracked pepper,
    plus a little extra to taste

Here's How:
You can use either an outdoor grill,
or a baking pan lined with foil and a
perforated insert that keeps the food from
falling to the bottom of the pan. If you are using a baking pan, make sure you are in a well-ventilated area without an overly sensitive smoke detector!

Soak some wood chips (any type you like) in water for at least 2 hours or overnight.

If you're grilling (you can use a commercial smoker too), heat up a small amount of charcoal, and after it is ready and hot, spread it to one side and scatter your wood chips on top of it. Place tomatoes away from direct heat and smoke for about 15-20 minutes or until skin is blistered and just starting to peel (remember, grills cook at different temperatures, so watch carefully and make sure your tomatoes don't start to peel and lose their juices).

If you're using a baking pan, place the tomatoes in the perforated insert and set aside. Then spread the wood chips on the foil in the bottom of your pan and place over medium-high heat. After the chips have started to smoke, place the tomatoes and perforated insert inside the baking pan. Cover with foil and poke a few holes to let the smoke escape. Cook for about 15 to 20 minutes, as described above.

When the tomatoes are done, let them rest for about 10 minutes before continuing. Then dice them, reserving the juices in a bowl.

Heat olive oil in saucepan over medium heat and then add the onions, garlic, bell pepper, jalapeno peppers and red pepper flakes. Cook until the vegetables are soft and fragrant, about 10 minutes. Add the tomatoes and their juices, along with the sugar.

Season with salt, pepper and cumin and cook for approximately 1 hour or more until the jam has a nice, thick consistency.

Cool completely. This will last for up to a month under refrigeration.

Part IV

GARLIC

❦

There is no such thing as a little garlic.

– Arthur Baer

29

GARLIC IN MY GENES

One of the very nicest things about life is the way we must regularly stop
whatever it is we are doing and devote our attention to eating.
— LUCIANO PAVAROTTI AND WILLIAM WRIGHT, *PAVAROTTI: MY OWN STORY*

I really can't pinpoint when I began my love affair with garlic, but I think it might be something I'm genetically predisposed to.

Growing up, my family ate bland, *real* bland. I came to that conclusion during my first quarter of college at Kent State University in 1978. With my little food coupons in hand, I slowly walked down the cafeteria line, in awe. There were stainless steel trays filled with incredible food, some I'd never seen before. What's manicotti? I asked innocently. In a state of pure delight I woofed down the ricotta-filled pasta shells before heading off to class.

I was dumbfounded when other students complained about the food. For me, this was culinary nirvana, but also an epiphany about the meals I'd eaten for the last 18 years, and the ongoing battles I'd had to change things in Mom's kitchen.

I was the cook for my two brothers and father when my mom worked second shift as a nurse.

There were three basic dishes I was required to prepare: either hamburgers, hot dogs or something we referred to as glop, which was overcooked macaroni with ground beef and tomato sauce. It was awful, but filling. No salt, no garlic and no flavor. Everyone would complain if I tried to spice the dishes up by adding garlic salt, herbs or some cheese. To this day the family is anything but adventurous at the dining table.

Married at 21, I was finally able to explore my fascination with cooking, and garlic became the basis for just about every dish I created – a tradition that has continued to this day.

But it wasn't until my late 20's that I learned the wonders of homegrown garlic and the secrets to growing it. I had tried unsuccessfully to grow it for two seasons and was lamenting the fact on the loading dock at The Youngstown Vindicator, the paper I worked for at the time.

One of the older printers was kind enough to explain everything I was doing wrong. I was planting in the spring and used store-bought garlic, just the antithesis of what I should have been doing. He proceeded to detail the proper procedures for planting that I still use today.

"Get local garlic," he said. "The stuff from the store isn't hardy and it's often treated with something that stops it from sprouting."

I ended up finding some garlic at a farmers market and used that to plant. These days I always order from Bobba-Mike's Gourmet Garlic Farm, which works wonderfully. I did a story on them years ago and love the quality and price of what they offer.

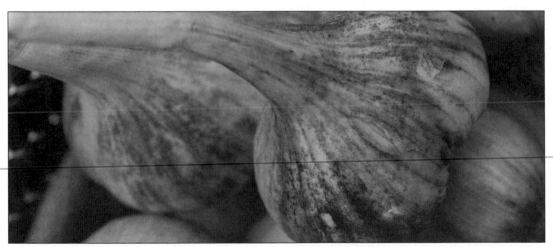

'Russian Giant' garlic might be the prettiest of them all. It produces large heads of four to seven cloves and has a wonderful mild flavor.

My friend on the loading dock told me to plant in the dark of the moon in the fall. That doesn't mean at night, that's the phase of the moon and is usually the second week of October. It's the perfect time for planting in zones 5 or 6. In cooler climates plant sooner, and the reverse for a warmer climate.

He told me that regardless of how deep I planted my garlic, if I did it during the dark of the moon, each head would be exactly six inches deep when harvested the next summer.

I took each head and separated the cloves, planting the biggest and saving the smaller ones for the kitchen. Each planted clove was supposed to become a head by next summer.

He sure seemed to be right about the harvest. I staggered the cloves, some deeper, some closer to the surface of the soft soil and they all were about the same depth when I pulled them.

Since then, I've planted garlic every fall. Sometimes I get it in the ground in September and other times it's not until November, but I always harvest nice big heads the next summer.

During a visit with Johno Prascak, a talented Pittsburgh artist, I was taken by something painted on his kitchen cabinet door. In beautiful white handwritten letters was this:

It would be a sad world without garlic.

I lay down on his kitchen floor, photographing the message that simply said it best. I knew then that we were kindred spirits and would always be linked by our love of garlic.

Garlic forms a connection, bonding friends and family. The smell of garlic hitting hot oil equates love in so many households. To those of us that can't get enough of the fragrance, it's an aroma that conjures up a lifetime of memories.

❧ IS GARLIC GOOD MEDICINE? ❧

Most people believe garlic is good for you; I sure do. I don't have a shred of scientific evidence, but that never stopped me before.

For thousands of years people have used garlic to cure everything from the common cold to the plague. Our word garlic comes from the old English word garleac, but the plant itself has been traced back 6000 years to central Asia.

Through the years garlic has been championed as a powerful curing herb that even has aphrodisiacal powers. Hippocrates used garlic vapors to treat certain types of cancer. A poultice made with garlic was used as an antibiotic to help heal wounds during World War II, when other medicines were hard to come by.

Garlic contains something called allicin that appears to have antibacterial properties, like a diluted penicillin.

It's also said to have antiviral uses too. Some people make a tea out of the herb for sore throats, but the list of remedies is long and curious, including treatments for athlete's foot and ulcers. Frankly I just like the taste, but I'll take any other benefits that happen to come with eating a few raw cloves.

There are some studies that show garlic can reduce bad cholesterol, and is a blood thinner that helps avoid clots. Those studies report that eating garlic regularly lowers blood pressure, prevents atherosclerosis (plaque in arteries) and reduces risk of heart attack or stroke, but as you might imagine, there's plenty of debate on all of this.

Nutritionally, garlic is high in manganese and vitamins B6 and C, and is a good source for selenium – with only about four calories per clove.

I can tell you from experience that eating lots of garlic helps keep the mosquitoes at bay too. They still want your blood, but they don't seem as voracious. It also repels people, which in many cases is a good thing, and as far as vampires go, I've never had one even come close.

There is one thing for sure: I feel better eating garlic, so that's got to be healthy, right?

30

Garlic Favorites

Have you heard about the garlic diet? You don't lose a lot of weight, but from a distance your friends will think you look thinner.
— AUTHOR UNKNOWN

Like any other crop, there are a lot of different kinds of garlic. I love tasting all the various subtleties on harvest day. Big cloves and tiny cloves, white, red and purple – each one offers something special.

It's been said that there are well over 500 types of garlic. Botanists call all garlic *Allium sativum*, but there are two subspecies: ophioscorodon, the hardneck varieties that send up a scape each summer, and sativum, the softneck garlics.

After that there's all sorts of groups – porcelain, rocambole, and several different purple striped varieties. No one's really sure how many, but I wish I could grow them all.

Softneck and Hardneck

You're most likely to find softneck garlic in groceries, because they can be planted mechanically, have tougher skin and keep better in storage – whereas hardneck garlic must be planted by hand, has thinner skin and is more sensitive to external conditions. Hardneck garlic has fewer, larger cloves and is the only kind that produces an edible seed head called a scape.

The garlic I plant is hardneck.

Once you figure out how easy garlic is to grow, the possibilities are yours to explore. I always find myself needing more space for garlic. It's easy to plant five pounds in a 30' x 40' garden (like mine) in the fall. But when spring comes, and you want to start planting all your other favorite things, will you be able to remember exactly where you planted those underground garlic bulbs back in September? Maybe, maybe not. That's why it's important to keep records.

✄ IT STARTS WITH A PLAN ✄

I always map out the garden for what's planned and then what actually gets planted – depending on what follows me home from the garden center. Spring planting can be confounding, as people give you this to plant or offer you that. Sometimes the plan needs to be revised.

It's actually fun for me to look at the plan I drew up last year when the garlic went in. With the precision of a city planner, I had carefully studied each square on the graph paper before I decided what should go where. Every square is up for consideration, the only constant being the plants that are perennial or winter over, like the garlic.

The main crop in my garden has been a variety called **'Music.'** It's very cold-hardy, a little spicy and filled with traditional flavor. 'Music' is easy to grow and stores well.

Picking the first few heads of 'Music' for the kitchen reminds the family what garlic is supposed to taste like. It produces four to six large cloves. They are easy to peel, have a shiny white sheath and a tinge of pink to their skins.

'German White' stands right behind 'Music' as a great white garlic. It's about the same size as 'Music' but a little spicier. Easy to grow, peel and very good for roasting.

'Spanish Roja' is one of the most popular of the red or purple garlics. It's smaller than the big white garlics, but what it lacks in size, it makes up in flavor. It forms eight to 12 reddish cloves that are easy to peel. It also stores very well.

'Chesnok Red' comes from Russia, making it very cold tolerant. It's packed with flavor and has a mellow aftertaste. It forms eight to ten red cloves and doesn't store as well as some of the others.

'Purple Italian' is another very popular garlic. It forms eight to ten deep purple cloves that are easy to peel. This one has a strong flavor that makes it perfect for Italian cooking.

'Georgian Fire' – I learned about this one from the great garlic author Chester Aaron (yes, there are great garlic authors). I hope you'll pick up a copy of *Garlic is Life*, one of his many excellent books. His writing is terrific, and not just about garlic.

In *Garlic is Life* he talked about 'Georgian Fire' and I had to have it – I still grow it today. It will wake you up, that's for sure. I love it raw in the garden. It produces about five medium-sized rose-colored cloves and it's filled with full-bodied flavor.

✄ MEET CHESTER AARON, A LEGEND IN THE GARLIC WORLD ✄

Reading his book, I found that Chester was from the Pittsburgh area, so I knew the *Post-Gazette* would be interested in doing an article on him.

In researching the author, I found out that just about every newspaper in the country had done something on him. Through his publisher, I tracked down his home number in California and got his answering machine.

It was Chester imitating Julia Roberts in the voice of Julia Child. It said something like, "Chester is out in the garden, and will call you back as soon as he can."

After hearing that high-pitched fake voice I knew this interview was going to be, er, different.

When he called back, Chester was overjoyed and near tears. "I used to deliver the *Post-Gazette*." He was thrilled that his hometown paper had finally found him. We talked for over an hour about garlic, which is scary in its own right. I learned a lot and found a kindred spirit who also enjoyed eating raw garlic right out of the garden.

I sent him my article after it was written. A couple of weeks later I got a FedEx box at the office from California. I held the box up to my nose and knew what was inside.

I ripped open the box and there were twenty different types of garlic. **'Beijing White'** was the first one I saw. There were a bunch of others I'd never even heard of – then I saw the Holy Grail of garlic, **'Transylvanian.'** Now there's a story to tell visitors to the garden, and that's something we all must do, bring people to see what we grow.

Chester is an icon on the West Coast when it comes to garlic, and I'm glad I was able to tell his story and eat his garlic.

> See Chester's recipe for Grilled Stuffed Trout (with garlic, of course), page 180; his Garlic Elixir, page 15; and his White Almond Garlic Soup with Grapes, page 183.

Some of the most incredible garlic varieties come from regular gardeners who have kept their garlic for generations. Every once in a while someone will contact me with a story about how this fabulous variety from the old country was brought over by a relative. They are priceless to their owners, but still they want to share. That's what gardening is all about.

It's great to try all these different varieties; like tomatoes, everyone has their own favorites. Explore, have fun and find yours. The journey can be a long one, but rewarding, as you taste clove after clove.

Cindy's Pizza Dough

It's always better when you make your own. This one's made with a bread machine.

What You Need:

¾ cup warm water
1 tablespoon olive oil
1½ teaspoon salt

2 ¼ cups all-purpose flour
1 teaspoon sugar
1 teaspoon yeast

Here's How:

Set to "dough only" setting, if that's available on your machine.

When done, remove the dough and put it on a floured board.

Press into a 12-inch thin crust. Now you're ready for the toppings and the oven!

Cindy's Garlic Pizza

I'm so blessed to have married a great Italian cook. One of my favorite dishes that Cindy makes is her rustic pizza covered in garlic. The recipe is simple but so tasty and it's always baked on a pizza stone. If you are interested in making pizza a regular part of your menu, I can't recommend enough the importance of investing in a pizza stone.

What You Need:

Splash of olive oil
1 cup red sauce
  (see recipe for Simple Red Sauce
  on page 74)
Pizza Dough (see recipe on page 169)

5 cloves fresh garlic
1 cup basil leaves
1 cup shredded mozzarella cheese,
  either the firm or fresh kind

Here's How:

Preheat the oven to 425°F.

Spread the dough out on baking stone with a little olive oil on the stone. Spread red sauce on the dough as thick as you would like.

Using a garlic press, squeeze the raw garlic over the red sauce. Spread the basil leaves on top of the garlic and red sauce and then sprinkle the cheese on top of everything.

Bake the pizza for 12 to 15 minutes until the crust is lightly browned.

Let the pizza stand for about 5 minutes before cutting and serving.

Produces one 12-inch pizza.

31

Planting Garlic

One of the most delightful things about a garden
is the anticipation it provides.
– W.E. Johns, *The Passing Show*, 1937

While down on my hands and knees for the annual fall ritual of planting garlic, I can't help but think of the three different harvests the plant will provide in the year ahead (and the endless winter I'll have to endure first, during its dormant period).

It's a pleasure planting in this soil. Like any other plant, garlic appreciates a place that's been worked up with lots of good organic matter. I use compost to build beds in the fall and then the garlic thrives.

✄ INSERTING THE CLOVES ✄

The cool, soft soil accepts the cloves as they are gently pushed into the ground, root side down. I space the cloves about six inches apart and plant about three inches down. These aren't exact measurements, and whether closer, farther away or deeper, the cloves will be fine.

It's the only time I don't water something right when I plant it. The fall rains will soak the soil soon enough.

Sometimes the plants even sprout before it gets really cold, but not to worry, the top growth will be killed off during the first deep freeze. I might even poach a few of the greens as an end-of-the-season treat. It will be five months until I'll be able to enjoy the spring treat again.

I tuck the garlic in for the winter with a thick layer of straw applied to the bed, which acts like a blanket and keeps the soil evenly moist.

❧ GOING FOR THE GREENS ❧

The greens will emerge right through the mulch when the crocus bloom. For a garlic lover like me, there's nothing like those greens.

They taste like garlic, but don't have the bite of the root. It's sheer pleasure to be standing in the cool spring rain savoring the greens. My wife always knows when the garlic is up – the telltale scent can't be hidden.

The greens can only be picked sporadically, as they provide energy to the bulb below. I like to reach down into the plant and pick the greens from the center. Early in the season they are firmer and more delightful, for some reason.

I've been having fun experimenting with growing the garlic only for its greens because I love them so. To do this I plant the cloves very close together, sometimes touching. I cover the bed with mulch and then a floating row cover, a lightweight spun bound translucent fabric that can be used as a season extender in the garden.

The greens will sprout at the same time as the uncovered plants, but grow quicker with the help of the cover.

Oftentimes, garlic will sprout where last year's plants were grown. Sometimes when the garlic is pulled it leaves behind a little castoff that waits until spring to emerge. Other times, it sprouts in the fall and can be enjoyed like the greens of spring.

They are wonderful additions chopped in salads, sauces and soups.

There can be no better treat in the garden than fresh garlic greens.

Garlic scapes are the seed head and stalk that emerges in early June from garlic plants. These plants are growing in my home garden in Western Pennsylvania.

✖ SECOND HARVEST: THE SCAPE ✖

This is the next harvest that garlic will provide. Since I grow hardneck varieties that put forth a scape (seed head), I know it's essential that the scape be removed so the plant can focus its energy into making big bulbs underground.

The scape begins to grow straight up from the center of the plant, then will turn, forming a loop. That's when I like to cut them, as close to the plant as possible.

Being someone who requires learning the hard way, I've left the scapes on some plants to see if in fact the bulbs were smaller at the end of the season, and in fact they were.

There are always a few scapes that I leave on, maybe three or four of the hundreds of plants I grow. They form a seed head filled with little garlic bulbets that are another garden treat.

Cut scapes left at room temperature will continue to swell and the tiny bulbets can be harvested from them too. The bulbets can actually be planted, but it takes years to make a nice sized head.

The scape is a seasonal delicacy prized in our home. I use it exclusively for making a pesto, substituting the scape for basil.

🐌 See Hazelnut Pesto with Garlic Scapes, page 179.

Scapes will store for months in the fridge and can be used for many recipes that call for the flavor of garlic. Describing the taste is like trying to explain what a sunset looks like: Trust me, if you like garlic, you'll like scapes.

🦋 THE FINAL HARVEST: WHEN AND HOW 🦋

This is what we've been waiting for, the big heads. Sometimes they are pure white; others have a tinge of purple or red. Each variety has a different taste. I love harvest day as I test each one in the garden for heat, texture and flavor.

> Garlic plants are ready to harvest when a little more than 50 percent of the greens have turned brown. It's important to harvest at the right time. Too early and the papery covering has not hardened, too late and the cloves will be too dry and fall apart in storage.
>
> Wait until a dry spell if possible; the bulbs will store better if allowed to dry out in the soil.

If the soil is soft, the plants can just be gently coerced out of the ground by tugging on the base of the plant. If the dirt is a little harder, take a fork, get under the bulb and pry it up to the surface.

Once they are free of their underground home, brush the dirt off the bulb and roots. I never hose them off unless I'm taking some inside to use right away in a recipe.

❧ STORING THE BULBS ❧

The longer the bulb stays attached to the greens, the better it will store. Hang them in a warm dry place for three weeks to cure.

The first time I visited Bobba-Mike's garlic farm, Bob and Wendy were curing their garlic in a big barn. Most people probably would have been repelled by the smell in there, but I went into a euphoric state, closing my eyes and breathing in the sweet scent of garlic; only a garlic lover could understand. Both of them knew we were on the same page. The three of us have been friends ever since – the bond of garlic again.

Someday I'm going to learn how to braid garlic. I look at the photos, read the tutorials, but mine look awful. I usually just give up and store the heads in onion bags.

They can store all winter if cured properly and often that's determined by the humidity during the process, something we can't control.

If they start to rot, you'll smell it. If that happens, take the good garlic that's left and chop it finely; add to some olive oil and freeze it right away. Note: Never, never, never store garlic in oil unless you're freezing it. Letting it stand in oil is a sure way to get botulism.

Garlic out of the garden is just like a tomato out of the garden: The taste can't be compared to store-bought. When those heads are peeled, chopped and cooked there's nothing better. When it's cooking in the kitchen, the smell drifts into the garden signaling me that it's time to finish up and get on inside.

Hazelnut Pesto with Garlic Scapes

This is a new take on an old favorite. I learned of this recipe from Pittsburgh chef Brandy Stewart while I was doing a story about garlic scapes – the tender, edible sprouts that come out of the garlic bulb. They usually have a milder flavor than the bulb. (Not sure how they got the name, but maybe it's because the sprouts 'scaped from the bulb…)

I love this different version of pesto using hazelnuts, safflower oil and Campo de Montalban cheese (a blend of cow's milk, sheep's milk and goat's milk, similar to Manchego cheese). It's a great example of how you can take a common recipe and switch it around, something I love doing and encourage you to do, too.

What You Need:

20 fresh garlic scapes in season.
  (Learn about scapes on page 176)
2 cups Campo de Montalban cheese, grated
½ cup hazelnuts
2 cups safflower oil

Optional: ½ cup good white wine
  (my wife eagerly offers this variation)
Salt and pepper to taste
1 pound pasta (I prefer linguini)
Drizzle of olive oil, to finish

Here's How:

Add scapes, cheese and nuts to a food processor and begin to process. Keep processing while adding the safflower oil and wine, a little at a time until you have reached desired thickness. Pesto can be served in a variety of consistencies, from very thick to rather thin, depending on preference.

Blend until smooth and paste-like, then season to taste with salt and pepper, and mix well.

Bring water to boil in a large pot, add pasta and cook until al dente. Add pesto to the pasta and finish with a drizzle of good extra-virgin olive oil.

Serves 4.

Grilled Stuffed Trout

Another recipe from my friend Chester Aaron. This one comes from his wonderful book, The Great Garlic Book (Ten Speed Press).

Trout is a mild, tender and flaky fish that does best with a simple recipe and fresh spices, like this one. Don't be afraid to cook fish whole – there's really nothing like the flavor and texture you'll get and you can easily remove the skin and bone before serving, if kids or spouses balk.

What You Need:

5 fresh or frozen trout (about ½ pound each)
Juice of 2 freshly squeezed lemons
2½ teaspoons salt
Freshly ground black pepper to taste
5 eggs, hard-boiled
¾ cup butter

12 cloves garlic, peeled and crushed or
   pressed (Chester recommends 'California
   Early' and 'Persian Star' varieties)
¼ cup fresh parsley, chopped
¼ cup fresh dill, chopped
1 teaspoon fresh thyme leaves

Here's How:

Clean trout and pat dry. Sprinkle both sides of each fish with lemon juice. Sprinkle ½ teaspoon salt on both sides of each fish and add a sprinkling of pepper. Put trout to the side while preparing the stuffing.

Grate the hard-boiled eggs into a bowl. Add the garlic cloves, then the parsley. Finally, add salt and pepper, to taste, and mix thoroughly.

Stuff each cleaned whole trout with the mix and then sprinkle with thyme. Chester recommends wrapping the trout in foil, though I often don't. Your call.

Roast on grill, 8 minutes each side.

Serves 5.

32

"What's That Smell?"

Three nickels will get you on the subway, but garlic will get you a seat.
— Yiddish saying

Garlic has always been a big part of life for my family. By the time my kids were walking they were enjoying copious amounts of garlic with every meal.

As my youngest son Matt got older, we enjoyed cooking together and would test the limits of both hot peppers and garlic. In the garden we would eat the hottest peppers, then run into the house and drink milk until the fire subsided. In the kitchen we would see how much garlic we could use in pasta dishes, often chopping two or three heads for a dish – and boy did we love it.

His girlfriend once asked him, "What *is* that?" – referring to the smell that is emitted by garlic lovers everywhere. The neighbors know when we eat dinner, as the aroma of cooking garlic drifts through the neighborhood every night around five.

My poor radio partner, Jessica Walliser, has to work in small production studios with me, which can cause an odiferous problem. Often, I ride my bike into the station, which just aggravates the situation.

After we had worked together for about six months we were cutting a segment in the tiny recording area and she started giggling. "What's up?" I asked. Being a polite person, she refused to answer. "Jess, we've been working together long enough, the honeymoon's over, what's the problem?" She blurted out, "You smell like an Italian sub sandwich." We both laughed, and you know what? She was right.

181

Another example of the power of garlic happened when my brother came over for a dinner and I wanted to see what he would do when confronted with a chicken dish dosed with lots of garlic.

Since "normal" people don't eat like my family, I thought this would be a fun experiment. He dug into the chicken and loved it, asking for seconds. He left that night, full and stinking of my beloved garlic.

Two days later his wife called saying, "What were you feeding him? It's coming out of his pores. He's been sleeping on the couch for two days."

I turned to my wife and said, "Honey, we really stink."

So, for all you garlic lovers out there, just be sure your significant other or family members eat some too, so you cancel each other out. It's only when you go out into the real world that there are problems.

White Almond Garlic Soup with Grapes

This is another old favorite from Chester Aaron. It's a chilled summer soup filled with unexpected – but perfect – flavors.

What You Need:

8 oz. blanched almonds, ground
3 slices white bread, crust removed
  and chopped
10 cloves garlic, peeled
  (Chester recommends 'Asian Tempest'
  or 'German Red' or 'California Late'
  varieties of garlic)

6 cups milk
2 teaspoons sherry vinegar
¾ cup extra virgin olive oil
Salt and freshly ground pepper to taste
36 white seedless grapes, sliced in half,
  for garnish

Here's How:

Mix almonds, bread, garlic, milk and vinegar in a blender at medium speed until well blended. Switch blender to high speed and slowly add olive oil until mixture is smooth. (If mixture tastes too strongly of either garlic or vinegar, add a small amount of water.)

Add salt and pepper to taste.

Chill soup for several hours. Serve in bowls with grape halves.

Serves 4 to 6.

33

GARLIC DISEASES

It takes a while to grasp that a garden isn't a testing ground for character
and to stop asking, what did I do wrong? Maybe nothing.

— ELEANOR PERÉNYI, *GREEN THOUGHTS*

When I contacted my friend, great garlic grower and author Chester Aaron in Occidental, California, he told me what started out as a sad story: He had lost 80 percent of his garlic to nematodes. When he told that story to another garlic farmer, word got around — and in no time, garlic growers from around the country had replaced his lost garlic stock with almost all of the rare varieties he had shared with them over the years. That's the power of the garden and that's the type of people who spend time with their hands in the dirt.

Garlic isn't bothered by many pests or diseases, but when one takes hold it can be devastating. Chester's nematodes are a rare but serious problem for a root crop like garlic.

Most garlic diseases are either in the soil or in the seed (bulb). They affect large fields, but can get into the garden. Rotating of the growing area and starting with good stock are the two most important ways to keep the garlic healthy. I've been lucky and have never had any problem with pests or diseases on my garlic and I've been growing it for over twenty years. Only twice have I heard of a gardener losing their crop to disease. The first was a call-in to my radio show, the second was Chester's story.

✼ THE BAD GUYS IN THE GARLIC PATCH ✼

Nematodes

These are tiny roundworms, microscopic actually. They live in the soil and plants and feed on the garlic bulb. It's important to be sure that any garlic you plant is not already infested with nematodes. Buying the bulbs from a good garlic farm is the first step.

> There's only one way to tell for sure if you've got nematodes, and that's to send a soil sample to a laboratory.

The symptoms include the stems and bulbs having a distorted and bloated tissue with a spongy look. The plants themselves will be stunted with short, thick leaves and many times have brown or yellow spots on them.

Dealing with nematodes organically is a challenge. Rotating crops will help. If you know you've got nematodes, don't grow garlic in the same place every year.

> If you've picked infested bulbs, try this: Soak the loose cloves at 100°F for 30 minutes in water containing 0.1 percent surfactant; then soak at 120°F for 20 minutes in the same kind of solution. Use a thermometer to monitor the water temperature. Then cool cloves in tap water for 10 to 20 minutes before drying in the oven for two hours at 100°F (start by setting oven at lowest setting, then let it cool a bit and throw in the garlic). This helps eradicate the bulb or stem nematode from loose cloves, though not from intact bulbs.

White Rot

White rot is a big problem on the West Coast, where much of the commercial garlic for the country is grown. But it can hit a garden patch too.

'Korean Red' garlic is a strong grower with just as strong flavor. It's colorful, hot and spicy. This one is great for cold climates.

It's especially a problem when things are cool in the spring. Symptoms include early yellowing of the foliage, stunted growth and dieback of older leaves, followed by the destruction of the root system and eventually the rotting of the bulb. Rotation is important. The disease can persist for a decade. Burn any plant that's infected.

One interesting control scientists are working on involves spraying a garlic extract on bare ground (where no garlic has been planted) in an area known to have white rot. This might stimulate the disease to grow and become exhausted before planting. Air temperatures for that procedure would have to be between 60°F and 70°F.

Fusarium Rot

This is a fungal problem that's present in all soils. It usually attacks plants that are weak or have been damaged or contracted another disease. The fungus thrives in hot weather. Removing infected plants as soon as discovered helps manage the disease. The hot water treatment above is said to reduce the possibility of the disease.

It looks a lot like white rot but progresses much slower and the plant can often survive. The bulbs could get worse during normal storage, so either use them right away or freeze the infected garlic to stop the disease's progress.

Downy Mildew

Another fungal disease, downy mildew symptoms include a whitish, furry growth on the leaves and yellow discoloration. Younger plants can be killed and the disease will stunt the growth of older plants. Bulbs in storage have a blackened neck, will be shriveled, and the outer scales will become water-soaked. Some bulbs may sprout prematurely.

Botrytis

Botrytis is sometimes called neckrot. In mild infections it might not even be noticed; when severe, the bulbs can rot. The fungus will attack garlic plants and bulbs after warm, wet weather. During cooler growing seasons, the disease may not be present, but can develop on stored bulbs. Bulbs in storage can degrade quickly if infected with the disease. Keep a close eye on them and if they start to rot, get them into the fry pan or the freezer.

Proper watering along with the suggestions above will prevent the disease. Soak the plants in the morning when needed and let them dry out during the day.

Penicillium Molds

These molds happen both in the garden and after the growing season, when the bulbs are in storage. Infected cloves planted in the fall can sprout in the spring, turn yellow and die. It's sometimes called blue mold because the cloves in storage have a bluish green color.

The simple control besides what's described above is not to plant bulbs with the mold.

Rust

Rust is another fungal issue that isn't likely in the garden, but has affected crops in the field in California. Small white flecks develop on the foliage, then progress to orange spots. The bulbs become shrunken and deformed. If hit hard, the plants can die.

Good cultural practices will keep your garlic going strong, but sometimes the weather or location can be the determining factor for the plants. Always start with good stock, that's the key.

One of many varieties of garlic, 'Italian Purple' is thought to come from Northern Italy and has a beautiful color. Try growing a couple of different types to see which one you love the best.

34

Garlic Pests

If I wanted to have a happy garden, I must ally myself with my soil...
— Marion Cran, *If I Were Beginning Again*

Garlic is a natural pesticide, so isn't affected by many insects. In my garden, I've never been bothered by any of the pests that can attack garlic and I've never heard of a home grower with pest problems, either. If you use the cultural practices detailed in the section on garlic diseases you should be fine. Take care of your soil and always make sure that compost and manures have broken down before using them in your garlic beds.

✄ HERE'S WHAT BUGS GARLIC ✄
(for the record)

Onion Maggots

These maggots start off as small flies tinier than houseflies. They lay eggs on the soil near germinating plants. After hatching, the larvae feed on the seedling and the bulb. They are a bigger problem for onions than garlic.

Bulb Mites

Bulb mites are tiny, shiny white mites that feed on the roots and bulbs of garlic. They can penetrate the outer skin of the garlic bulb and cause it to rot. They are most prevalent in cool, wet weather.

Thrips

More of a problem for onions than garlic, thrips are another tiny pest that is hard to see. It takes a magnifying glass to see that they are yellow or brown and have two pairs of wings. They love hot and dry weather and are the biggest problem in areas that favor those conditions.

They can be controlled by natural predators and Spinosad.

The Pea Leafminer

The pea leafminer first shows up as eggs laid inside the leaf tissue. They hatch to form larvae that tunnel inside the leaves. They leave the plant when the pest becomes an adult. Full-grown leafminers are small black and yellow flies. The damage to the plants is usually just cosmetic.

Wheat Curl Mites

These are hard to spot and usually don't damage garlic unless there's a severe infestation. When that happens the leaves will be streaked and twisted and the overall growth of the plant will be stunted. But where we see the main damage from the mite is in storage. It can cause cloves to dry out.

Frankly, I wouldn't worry about any of these pests. Start with good soil, good garlic seed, rotate crops and your garlic patch should be fine.

Storage Tips

Don't store garlic in the refrigerator or in a plastic bag. It will become moldy.

Do store garlic in a cool, dry place out of the sunlight. It likes air circulation, so consider using a "garlic keeper" pot, which has holes to allow for air circulation and also looks very nice on your countertop.

"Onion snow" – that's what we call it here in Pennsylvania, when an early spring snow lays a white blanket over the dark green tips of our onions and garlic.

Leg of Lamb Stuffed with Basil and Garlic

This recipe is a little more difficult than others here, but it's worth it, and not really that complicated. With lamb, basil and garlic how can you go wrong? It's another dish that needs to be started the night before. Don't skimp on the marinating time, because it's that overnight soaking in the wonderful liquid that makes all the difference. Based on a recipe from The New American Cheese by Laura Werelin (Henry N. Abrams).

What You Need:

1 leg of lamb, boned and butterflied (This works out to about 3 to 4 pounds of meat.)
1½ cups good red wine
4 tablespoons olive oil
6 cloves fresh garlic, minced
1 tablespoon fresh oregano leaves, chopped
1 tablespoon fresh basil leaves, chopped
2 whole heads of garlic
6 oz. feta cheese, crumbled
2 tablespoons milk

1 red bell pepper, roasted, skinned and cut lengthwise into strips
15 to 20 whole basil leaves
kitchen string
1½ pounds small creamer potatoes (about 18 potatoes cut in half, or use about 9 larger red potatoes cut into quarters)
1 tablespoon all-purpose flour
½ cup unsalted lamb, chicken or beef stock
Sea salt and freshly ground pepper to taste

Here's How:

To butterfly the lamb (removing the bone):

Using a sharp knife, cut a slit down to the bone on the side where it is closest to the surface, and then cut it out carefully. You'll also need to remove the kneecap. When you're done, a thick vein of fat will become exposed. Cut that out too.

Place the butterflied lamb in a large baking dish.

Mix together 1 cup of the wine, olive oil, garlic, oregano, and chopped basil, and salt and pepper, to taste. Pour the mixture over the lamb and cover it. Place in refrigerator overnight, up to 24 hours.

On day 2, allow the lamb to come to room temperature, which will take about an hour.

While you're waiting, roast the garlic using the technique described on page 125, and then squeeze it out into a bowl. Mix in the feta, milk and a little freshly ground pepper until creamy.

Preheat the oven to 500°F – some ovens won't get quite that high, so just get it as close as you can.

Discard all but about 1/4 cup of the lamb marinade, then lay the lamb out on a cutting board. Score the meat to make rolling easier.

Place the red pepper strips down the middle of the lamb, leaving some space around the edges. Place the whole basil leaves on top of the peppers. Gently spread the feta garlic mixture on top of the peppers and basil.

Roll the lamb up, tying it together with kitchen string.

Now place the lamb in a baking dish. Arrange the potatoes around the sides and pour the remaining 1/4 cup of marinade over the lamb and potatoes, making sure that everything is well coated. Add plenty of salt and pepper to the meat.

Roast at the highest temperature for 10 to 5 minutes, then reduce the heat to 425°F and cook for 30 to 40 minutes until the meat is medium rare (160°F on a meat thermometer).

Let the roast stand for 10 to 15 minutes.

While you're waiting, prepare the sauce:

Put 4 tablespoons of liquid from the baking dish into a saucepan. While stirring quickly, add the flour and the rest of the wine. Bring to boil. Cook 1 minute.

Slice the lamb and pour sauce on top.

Serves 6 to 8.

Garlic on harvest day in July – my favorite photo.

Part V

BASIL

I asked the boy beneath the pines.
He said, "The master's gone alone
Herb-picking somewhere on the mount,
Cloud-hidden, whereabouts unknown.
– Chia Tao (777-841)

Large-leaved 'Genovese' basil is a favorite in the garden, great for stuffing and all recipes.

35

FOR THE LOVE OF BASIL

"A man taking basil from a woman will love her always."
— SIR THOMAS MORE, STATESMAN IN THE COURT OF HENRY VIII

Just brushing against a basil plant releases the unmistakable aroma that means summer. The garden isn't complete without basil. It's so easy to grow, harvest and use in recipes. Basil is the king of the herb garden, providing its remarkable flavor all summer long.

I love to pick the tops of the plant and just hold them to my nose, enjoying the intoxicating fragrance and knowing soon the fresh treat is bound for the kitchen. In fact, basil's trademark aroma is actually biblical: Salome hid the head of John the Baptist in a pot of basil to mask its decomposing odor. Now that's an herb with a strong aroma – and other, more pleasant, uses.

Fresh is everything for basil. It doesn't translate well as a dried herb; it's certainly something completely different when not picked right from the garden.

Basil is a member of the mint family with the botanic name *Ocimum basilicum*. Over the centuries, basil has been used for many things, including as a preservative in the mummies of ancient Egypt.

It has long been known to help digestion, and the oil enhances dull skin, relieves stress, improves circulation – and does a host of other helpful things. Oh yeah, and it tastes good too.

We often equate basil with Italy, where it can mean love. Suitors wear a sprig of the herb in their hair when courting. Other on the other hand, ancient Greeks and Romans thought basil would only grow if you screamed wild curses and shouted while planting the seeds (gardening is supposed to be therapeutic, right?).

I rarely yell at my plants or seeds, preferring to use a carrot instead of a stick to make them grow. I do talk to them and even sing to them and they reward me with wonderful harvests each summer.

If you can, grow some basil somewhere in your garden. It will reward you time after time with its sweet scent and wonderful flavor. There's a variety for every application in the kitchen and the garden. Each one has a little different flavor and they're fun to experiment with.

Basil is an herb that can be overused without worry. It's such a mild, pleasurable flavor that it's hard to use too much.

❧ WHO'S WHO IN THE BASIL FAMILY ❧

The basil varieties range from huge green-leafed plants to tiny globes perfect for containers.

'Lettuce Leaf' or 'Green Ruffles' basil is one of my favorites. It produces huge green leaves that are perfect for stuffing with some Italian gorgonzola goat cheese and sliced cherry tomatoes – or a little Prosciutto...but more about recipes later.

'Genovese' basil is the standard basil you'll find in most stores. It has big leaves (but not as big as 'Lettuce Leaf') and offers the traditional basil flavor.

'Spicy Globe' basil forms tiny neat bush-like plants with small leaves. It's great for growing in containers or windowsills indoors at the end of the season. It can be used like its bigger cousins.

'Lemon' basil is a different species that smells like lemons and is sweeter than other cultivars. It works well with chicken dishes and has many other uses.

'Thai' basil has more of a licorice or anise flavor and is used in Asian cooking, but don't limit the herb to that. Have fun and experiment with it in other recipes. Some people describe the flavor as warm or peppery.

'**African Blue**' basil is an ornamental, vigorous grower. The leaves are bluish-green with a soft texture and lavender flowers.

'**Cardinal**' is a really cool basil sold by Burpee. It flowers in deep burgundy and could looks beautiful grown alongside a bed of ornamental flowers.

'**Cinnamon**' basil has violet stems and lavender flowers. It offers a slight cinnamon flavor that's good with Asian or Middle Eastern cooking.

'**Lime**' basil has the flavor of lime, with white flowers and is great for fruit dishes.

'**Osmin Purple**' basil is for eating, and not an ornamental variety. It's got one of the darkest purple leaves and stems. Small, sweetly scented leaves are a wonderful accent for salads and other dishes.

'**Nufar**' basil is the first variety of 'Genovese' basil to be resistant to fusarium wilt. Tastes like its cousin, but disease-resistant. What's not to like?

There are even more varieties, so if you're a basil nut like me, get to the nursery and see what you can find.

✄ GROWING BASIL FROM SEEDS ✄

Once you've decided what kind you want to grow – and you might want to try lots at once – it's time to get those seeds started.

Growing basil from seeds is simple, if you use the same techniques I wrote about in "A Passion for Seeds" (Chapter 23) in the tomato section. Remember, after seeds germinate indoors, they'll need to be grown under bright light, like a fluorescent shop light left on for 24 hours a day.

> It's very important not to overwater your seedlings, as they will succumb to fungal disease.

Out in the garden, basil grows best in good soil improved by organic matter. They can be spaced at 12 inches and will form bushy plants in full sun. Wait until all chance of frost has passed, as the herb is very tender. Let the soil warm up first; basil loves it hot, just like tomatoes.

Sometimes I'll buy 12-inch-high plants in pots with four or five plants in the same pot. They are so big that they would be hard to divide. I plant them as is, and harvest once they get going, eventually thinning the plants down to one per pot.

Sowing Directly Into the Garden

Yes, you can do it this way, too. First thing in the season, once the soil is warm enough, I plant out basil plants, and at the same time I plant some seed for a later harvest. When the plants start to get tired at the end of the season, the basil grown from seed will be just hitting its stride.

> If you do indoor germinating as well as direct sowing, you have the option of creating your own staggered timing throughout the season.

Protect Against Frost and Bugs

Early in the season, the plants can be covered with a floating row cover to protect them from cool temperatures. It will also prevent the four-lined plant bug from getting to the plants. The pest attacks the new sprouts and foliage at the top of the plant, covering it with brown pockmarks.

Keep 'Em Comin'

To keep your plants producing, trim off the flowers, which are edible. Getting to the top leaves before flowering will keep the plants going. My own garden can't provide the sun the plants really need, but they still produce just fine. They just grow a little differently, tall and thin instead of stout and bushy.

About those flowers: I love them chopped finely in salads. They can be used in any basil recipe for a little different taste and texture.

Now For the Best Part...Did Someone Say "Pesto"?

Nothing can evoke the feeling that basil does when it's brought into the kitchen and used fresh as a garnish or cooked with a recipe.

Rarely is basil the main ingredient of the meal, but part of the supporting cast that can make the dish a star.

Italian cuisine is where basil is most renowned. It's hard to beat the simple triumvirate of tomatoes, garlic and basil – combined with good olive oil. The herb's signature dish, though, might be pesto. Mixed with olive oil, Parmesan cheese and usually pine nuts, it's a great classic topping for pasta.

'Lemon' basil going to seed. This basil has a hint of lemon. It's great to use in seafood dishes.

Goat Cheese and Pesto Puff Pastry

There's something about using puff pastry with savory dishes that makes a meal seem fancy. I serve this one to guests all the time.

What You Need:

1 pack ready-rolled puff pastry
2 tablespoons pesto (see recipe for
  Mortar and Pestle Pesto on page 209)
1¼ oz. feta or goat cheese, crumbled
(feta will make a saltier, sharper tasting pastry;
goat cheese will be milder)

1 cup cherry tomatoes, halved
1 tablespoon fresh basil, roughly chopped
Pepper, to taste.

Here's How:

Preheat the oven to 400°F.

Take one sheet of puff pastry and cut it into fours,

Place the four pieces on a parchment-lined baking sheet.

With small knife, make a slit about ½ inch in from the edge all the way around each pastry. Do not cut through all the way.

Place a dollop of pesto on each pastry and spread to the line you just cut.

Place the tomato halves on the pesto – go ahead and cram as many as you like onto the pastry.

Put the baking sheet in the oven for 10 minutes and then add the feta or goat cheese and a sprinkling of fresh ground black pepper.

Return to the oven for another 8 minutes. Serve warm.

Makes 4 pastries.

'Spicy Globe' basil up close. Its tiny fragrant leaves have the same bold flavor as larger-leaved basil.

36

STORING AND PRESERVING BASIL

*Gardening with herbs…is indulged in by those who like
subtlety in their plants in preference to brilliance.*

— HELEN MORGENTHAU FOX

There's a certain point in the season, usually the first night that frost is pre-dicted, when gardeners realize it's time to save the basil that's left in the garden.

That might mean a mad dash into the garden after the weather forecast – or it might be a planned trip to the garden a week earlier, for those who know it's time to put the warm-temperature-loving plant out of its misery.

Storing basil and keeping that wonderful flavor alive for as long as possible can be a challenge.

Drying

For me, drying is the last choice; it will do in a pinch if you don't have the real thing handy to grab an aromatic leaf from. That's why I grow it downstairs all winter, under fluorescent lights.

But if you choose to preserve your plants by drying, pull them out of the garden before any chance of frost. The slightest hint of frost will turn them black and they will be useless to you.

Three Ways You Can Dry Basil

- Hang them upside down in bunches in a cool, dry place. To prevent the plants from turning brown, just separate the plants with thin layers of newspaper, and then hang them with a string or wire. The paper somehow helps keep the color in the plants – something to do with oxidation, I think.

  Or...

- Lay the plants on a wire rack outside in the shade.

  Or...

- Dry them in the oven. Preheat it to 350°F, then strip the stems of the leaves and put them on a baking sheet. It takes five or ten minutes to dry. When properly dried, the leaves will easily crumble between your fingers.

The leaves can be left whole or crumbled to fine dust, depending on how you like to use them. Store the dried herb in an airtight container. I use plastic zipper bags when I have dried basil, but anything will work.

Other Methods of Preserving Fresh Basil

Any preserving method is meant to keep as close as possible to the taste of fresh. Here are a few more:

- Freezing is the method I prefer for saving basil over the winter months. It can be as simple as putting some basil in an ice cube tray with water, or just taking the leaves and putting them in a zipper bag in the freezer.

  I like the ice cube tray; you can just pop out the cube and throw it into sauce or soup. Be aware that basil loses its texture when frozen, but it will retain much of its distinctive flavor.

My favorite way to freeze the herb is to put it into a food processor with some olive oil to make a sort of basil paste. This mixture can be put into ice cube trays too. It works pretty well for pesto and it's great for all sorts of other dishes. When you drop a couple of cubes into a saucepan filled with hot garlic, it will make your heart beat faster.

- For storing in the refrigerator, here is an interesting way to keep leaves, using salt as a preservative. This method might be the most like just-picked basil. It goes back decades or more. You take a lidded glass jar and layer basil leaves with sea salt inside, being careful that the leaves aren't touching. I start with a half inch of salt, then some leaves, more salt and so on.

Secure the lid and you'll be pleasantly surprised how long the leaves will last, maybe until next spring. They become a little papery, but retain some texture and fresh flavor. As the leaves are used, the salt can be used for seasoning all sorts of food.

> Don't even think about storing a basil and oil mixture in the fridge! There's a chance of botulism, so that shouldn't be an option.

One of the most convenient ways to store the basil is by turning the last crop into pesto. Pesto just means a combination of oil, cheese, nuts and greens; in this case, basil is the green. The most popular way to make it is with olive oil and pine nuts, but there are a thousand variations. Don't be afraid to experiment during the season, perfecting a recipe that can be used to save the basil for as long as possible.

Once the pesto is created, it can be frozen and used for a year in different recipes.

> The English food writer Patience Gray once wrote: *Pounding fragrant things is a tremendous antidote to depression.*

❧ POUNDING FRAGRANT THINGS ❧

I was in an antique store a few years ago with my dearest friends who were visiting from out of town. I saw an old mortar and pestle that I had to have. The shopkeeper asked if I was a pharmacist, and I said no, I just love to cook.

Anyone who's ever made traditional pesto knows that the best way to combine the ingredients is the old-fashioned way, with mortar and pestle. There's something deeply satisfying about using the tool in the kitchen. It's something I use a lot for making pesto or combining garlic and salt to be used in a sauce.

Working with your hands to get the consistency just where you want is as fun as it is gratifying. It's not something that can be done every day, but a special dinner takes time and there's nothing like spending a little extra time to make it extra special. Use the blender if you must for every day preparations, but once in a while let yourself take a step back in time.

🔖 See the two pesto recipes: Mortar and Pestle Pesto (page 209); and Hazelnut Pesto with Garlic Scapes (page 179).

It's cathartic to stand looking out the kitchen window slowly grinding the ingredients into the perfect mix. Life's short; an hour in the kitchen working with basil, oil, salt and some pine nuts or hazelnuts puts a smile on my face every time.

Mortar and Pestle Pesto

This classic Italian sauce calls for Parmigiano Reggiano cheese, which Chef Mario Batali calls the king of cheeses – and I agree.

What You Need:

4 cloves fresh garlic
2 cups basil leaves
1 teaspoon sea salt
Freshly ground pepper to taste
½ cup of the best extra-virgin olive oil
  (or safflower oil for something a little lighter)

⅓ cup pine nuts
  (or hazelnuts for an updated flavor)
¾ cup of grated Parmigiano Reggiano
2 tablespoons unsalted butter at
  room temperature
  to better blend with the other ingredients

Here's How:

Combine the garlic and salt and work until smooth, with the pestle rubbing against the mortar. Then add the nuts and continue the grinding process. Add half the basil and half the oil and work into a paste-like texture. Then add the rest of the basil and oil and keep combining.

Put the mixture in a bowl and add the cheese and butter and thoroughly mix.

Serve over pasta or on bread.

Serves 4.

Pasta Sauce with Thyme

How about an easy recipe for when you have more tomatoes than you know what to do with? This deliciously different sauce goes perfectly over pasta shells.

What You Need:

3 teaspoons olive oil
4 garlic cloves, coarsely chopped
3 pounds tomatoes, cut into wedges
1 sprig fresh thyme
¼ cup dry white wine

½ cup chicken stock
1 cup basil chiffonade
1 cup pasta shells, cooked al dente
Sea salt and freshly ground black pepper

Here's How:

Prepare your pasta shells according to the instructions on the package. While it's cooking, start your sauce.

In a large skillet, heat the oil over medium heat. Add the garlic and sauté until it begins to turn gold, about one minute.

Increase the heat to medium high and add the tomatoes and thyme. Cook, stirring gently, until the skin begins to loosen from the tomatoes – about 2 minutes.

Add the wine and cook 1 minute more. Add the chicken stock and simmer for about 2 minutes. Season with salt and pepper.

Remove the thyme and ladle the sauce into serving bowls over the pasta. Garnish with the basil leaves.

Serves 4 to 6.

37

STEPHANIE'S BASIL STORY

*Gardens are like daughters: They fill the world with beauty,
and sometimes attract pests.*

— AUTHOR UNKNOWN

For as long as I can remember, I've been feeding things to my kids right out of the garden.

Everyone finds their favorites, and even today at ages 20, 22 and 24 they ask for certain things, but still don't understand what's ready when. I can get a request for snow peas in July or tomatoes in May. All they know is that sometime after winter, food starts magically appearing in the kitchen.

One summer, when my daughter Stephanie was a young child, she was spending some time out in the garden with me. We tasted and tried all sorts of things. At the height of basil season we took the leaves and crushed some fresh 'Georgian Red' garlic into the leaves. (That red garlic has its own distinct flavor that I treasure.)

Stephanie was always up for anything and will tell you definitively whether she loves something or hates it. The basil and garlic was a hit. It was wonderful just sitting in the warm sun on the grass with her, nibbling treats that would make us smell for a couple of days at least.

As gardeners, one of the most wonderful things we do is share what we grow, especially with someone who can appreciate it.

Steph picked up on that right away, sensing the pleasure I had in feeding her the soft green leaves with the earthy garlic that had a bite to it.

I think it was the next day that my wife Cindy and I were going for a walk in the garden and ran into Steph standing in between the house and the garden with a big smile on her face as she chewed on some greens.

"I found some basil," she said happily. In horror I looked at what she was eating and yelled "That's not basil, it's poison ivy!"

She looked at me, scared, with those big innocent eyes, with part of a poison ivy vine hanging out of her mouth, and started spitting out the vile plant. We ran into the house and scrubbed her hands and face, paying special attention to her mouth.

Amazingly, she never had an adverse reaction to the poison ivy. It's become one of her favorite garden stories to tell about her youth.

Now, when kids visit the garden I warn them with that tale, and feel very old as I stress the importance of asking Mom and Dad before they pick or eat ANYTHING. The garden can provide the tenderest treats filled with fresh flavor, but even the forest can fool the most discerning of palates.

POISON IVY AND POISON OAK – PLAYING IT SAFE

My radio partner Jessica Walliser has a great way to pull up the vines. Take a large garbage bag and pull it over your arm. Now you can grab a vine or vines and then pull the bag back over the offensive weed. By never touching the leaves or vine, hopefully the itchy oils won't come in contact with your skin. If you do find yourself infected with poison ivy there's no cure, but there are ways to treat the rash, and one of the most effective I've found is called Tecnu Extreme Medicated Poison Ivy Scrub. It's available at most drug stores. Jess and I gave it away to listeners and people loved it. I've recommended it to countless friends who welcomed relief from the pain and itch of poison ivy.

38

GROWING BASIL INDOORS

"[M]ark this curious herb... Touch it lightly, stroke it softly,
and it gives forth an odor sweet and rare."
— CHARLES GODFREY LELAND, *SWEET BASIL*

Many herbs can be brought in and grown on the windowsill at the end of the season. Basil is not one of them. It will limp along, get leggy, then eventually give up the ghost.

But that doesn't mean there's no way to grow the plant inside. The key is to start them inside from seed, cuttings or small plants and put them under a good light source.

The first and most obvious way to get plants at the end of the season is to take cuttings from an existing plant. This means making more plants from the same plant, and it's pretty easy.

✄ TAKING CUTTINGS ✄

You'll need some scissors, small pots, enough plastic to cover the containers, some vermiculite or perlite – and a rooting hormone; Rootone is a powdered form, the organic version is made out of willow (one brand is called Green Light).

For do-it-yourselfers, you can make your own rooting solution by soaking some yellow-tipped shoots from a weeping willow tree. Soak the shoots until the water becomes the color of tea.

You can make another very effective organic rooting solution out of honey: Boil two cups of water and add a tablespoon of honey. Let the mixture cool, then store in an airtight container in a dark, cool place. Use it as you would any other rooting solution. It will last a couple of weeks until a new solution needs to be mixed.

Any one of the rooting mediums will work to propagate your cuttings. Then fill some small pots with vermiculite or perlite. I like three-or-four-inch plastic containers.

How To Do It

To take the cuttings, just cut off the tips of the basil plants about two or three inches from the top. I was always taught to cut the branches at a 45-degree angle to allow more surface area to root, but horticulturalists have told me that really doesn't make a difference. Strip off all but the top leaves and dip the bottom of the stem in a rooting medium.

Now place the cutting into the pot filled with the vermiculite or perlite. Cover the pot(s) with plastic and keep them in a place that doesn't get too hot, and away from direct sunlight.

In a couple of weeks, gently tug on the plants. If they resist, they have started to root. If that's the case they can be potted up into a good organic planting mix and grown under lights.

Growing Under Lights

My favorite lights are simple fluorescent shop lights hung on chains above a table in the basement. The lights are hung a couple of inches above the plants. In the chapter about growing tomatoes from seed, I mention another good trick, which is to surround the plants with aluminum foil to use reflected light to keep the plants growing strong.

In my basement growing operation I leave the lights on 24/7. The plants do fine, since the fluorescents aren't nearly as strong as the sun.

Note: An important job each season is to change the fluorescent bulbs. You might be able to use them in other parts of the house, but one year of running all day and night pretty much wears them out. We can't see the difference, but the plants sure can.

Starting With Seeds

I love to take cuttings at the end of the season, but I also start some seeds in pots and put them under the lights. I can't be without fresh basil long or I go crazy, and that ain't pretty.

The seeds are easy to start if you follow the basic steps outlined earlier in the book for tomato seeds. Your basil seeds will sprout in a little over a week.

Thinning

Whether you are growing basil in pots or out in the garden, you will sometimes need to pull out the most crowded plants in order to let the stronger ones have more room to thrive.

I can't stand to waste plants that are thinned, when there are a couple of good ways to use them. Sometimes, with small seedlings, I replant them in pots in the planting mix. When they are moved right after sprouting, they respond well to transplanting.

But the thinnings can also be used like most other tasty edibles; just throw them in a salad. They are so tender and bursting with flavor, they light up the salad and melt in your mouth.

There's always a chance of finding some small plants in a nursery at the end of the season. If they grow their own stuff, see if they would start a few basil plants for you.

Best Indoor Varieties

There are certain varieties of basil that lend themselves to indoor growing under lights.

    'Spicy Globe' basil stay compact like a little round meatball shrub.

    'Dwarf' basil and **'Green Bouquet'** and **'Bush'** basil are also good choices.

'Spicy Globe' basil growing in a pot with lettuce and a geranium.

'Dwarf Greek' basil is a cool heirloom variety offered by Baker Creek Heirloom seeds. It only gets six inches high, which is perfect for indoor growing.

But full sized plants will work too. I just hack them back so they don't get too tall. I don't like to let them grow above 12 inches, because it's hard to get enough light on them to keep them from getting leggy.

Care and Feeding

In my operation I've got an old large stainless steel darkroom sink filled with water. When the plants get dry I just set them in there for an hour or so until they soak up what they need.

A word of warning: Most indoor plants are killed with kindness, so don't overwater or over-fertilize.

It's better for the plants to be allowed to dry out a little bit. Since basil is prone to fungal diseases, a little dry as opposed to soaking wet is beneficial.

I like to use a water-soluble fertilizer every two weeks mixed at full strength to keep the plants growing strong.

Your plants will last for months while being harvested. I'll take some cuttings off the plants as they get older, and pot them up and let them have a second or third life, to keep me happy in the kitchen.

I use the cutting techniques above and just keep them under the lights until they root, then pot the basil up and keep it growing until it's time to start my tomatoes, peppers and other summer plants.

It's not until the end of the winter that the basil plants are relegated to the windowsill, where they sulk while being harvested during their last days.

Bring your love of basil inside. The sweet aroma reminds us of long summer days and fresh tomato sauce.

Easy Baked Basil Fries

I love potatoes and basil together. There are endless possibilities with this combination, but I love this quick and easy side dish.

What You Need:

½ cup Parmigiano Reggiano cheese, grated
4 tablespoons olive oil
½ cup basil leaves, chopped

5 cloves of fresh, minced garlic
4 medium red potatoes, cut into thin slices

Here's How:

Preheat oven to 400°F.

In a bowl, combine the cheese, oil, basil and garlic.

Add the potatoes to the cheese mixture and mix until the potatoes are covered with the mix.

Spread on a baking sheet and cook for 40 to 50 minutes, turning once.

Serves 4.

SAVING BASIL SEEDS

And the earth brought forth grass, and herb yielding seed
after his kind…and God saw that it was good.
– GENESIS 1:12

Even though it's standard procedure to remove the flower spike from basil plants to encourage leaf growth, some of us can't resist leaving the spike on a few of our plants so the flowers will produce seeds we can save for next year.

Seed saving is fun, easy and it saves money for next year's crop.

The first rule of saving seed for any plant is to identify the plants as open pollinated or hybrid. Most basils are open pollinated, but some newer varieties are hybrids.

The Problem with Hybrid Seeds

Hybrid plants (as explained in Chapter 25) are plants that are crossed to create a certain variety. Breeders select for particular traits and by crossing two parents, try to highlight that trait or traits.

Seeds from hybrids will not grow true; they revert to one of the parents. Sometimes the seeds will be sterile and won't germinate at all.

Determining if a plant is hybrid or open pollinated is easy as long as you keep the plant tag or note the fact when the plant is bought. Hybrids are always labeled as such, and if they aren't, then you can assume the plant you're looking at is open pollinated.

Even though you don't get the same plant when hybrid seeds are saved, it can be a fun experiment to find out what sprouts. Since a basil plant is grown mainly for its foliage, it's pretty easy to see what it will look like early on in the growing season. But really, have you ever seen a basil you didn't like?

One type of basil can cross-pollinate with another, so if you're saving seed, separate the basil types by at least 150 feet. Or let them cross and see what nature creates. Maybe you'll discover the next great basil.

Timing

The best way to save seeds is to let a couple of plants go to seed and save from the one that bolts last. That way you're saving the favorable trait of later seed production. The later a plant goes to seed, the more time it spends growing nice, big leaves to harvest.

The seed stalks emerge from the center of each branch and form a long truss of flowers, then seeds.

The trick is to harvest the seeds right before the plant releases them to the ground – and that takes practice. You want mature seeds. Fully-grown seeds will do best for you the next year; harvest too early and you might be stuck with low germination or plants without good vigor.

Watch the plant, and as the flower stalk turns brown and begins to dry, the seeds will start to mature and harden.

Stripping the Pods

The seedpods can be stripped from the stalk easily and then dried in a paper bag or on a plate. When they're dry, just roll them around with the palm of your hand on a cutting board and the seeds will fall out.

It's optional to remove the chaff. I always do. I want the seed separated out so that there's no variable during storage.

Winnowing

Once the seeds and chaff dry, a process called winnowing is used to separate the two.

Pick a day when there's a nice breeze but not monsoon winds. Take two bowls and place the seed and chaff in one of them.

Hold the filled bowl in one hand a foot or so above the empty bowl, which you hold in the other hand. Now tip the filled bowl, dropping the chaff and seed into the other bowl and repeat. Since the chaff is lighter than the seed, some of the chaff will "winnow" away in the wind.

Do this enough times and eventually all you'll be left with is seed. I remember the first time I winnowed – I thought all the seed would be lost in the wind, but it worked. The chaff floated away, actually ending up on my patio and requiring a bit of a cleanup.

Be sure to label the seeds with the variety and date saved and any other pertinent notes.

> Proper storage of the seed is crucial to keeping it viable and happy. The most important thing is that once the seed is dry, you'll want it to stay dry.

Drying

There's a couple of ways to get the seed dry for storage. I use silica gel in the bottom of mason jars. It has little colorful specks that let you know when it's absorbed moisture. When they change color, the silica gel can just be dried down in the oven or microwave. You want to start with gel that is as dry as possible.

When the silica gel is completely dry the indicators are deep blue. When it absorbs moisture it changes from blue to pink. Heating the gel drives out the absorbed moisture, and the color of the indicators returns to blue.

I bought my silica gel from a craft store in a one-gallon container and it was cheap. I used some to fill the bottom of my seed-saving mason jars and some to dry flowers with.

I like to dry mine in the oven. Pre-heat it to 275°F and put the silica gel into a baking pan. Note to guys: you might not want to tell your wife you're putting this in the oven – but there's nothing to worry about. The gel will turn blue in an hour or two depending on how much is being dried.

For the microwave, put the silica gel into a container that's safe for this type of use. Set the power to medium and dry the gel for around five minutes. Stop the process at about two minutes to stir and inspect the gel. Continue the process until the gel turns blue taking care not to overcook the drying agent.

Storing

I store the seeds in paper envelopes put into the mason jars, with about a half inch of gel at the bottom. I put them in a cool, dark place. For me that's the basement. If you can find a spot that's around 50°F that never freezes, that's perfect.

Some seed savers freeze their seed; I don't like to. I always worry there might be too high a moisture content in the seed, and in certain seeds, the seed coat can crack when frozen.

'Genovese' basil sends up a flower stalk that can be pinched off so the plant will keep putting on its tasty, aromatic foliage. The edible flowers can make an interesting addition to dishes in the kitchen.

If the basil seed is stored correctly it will last for years. When I get about five seasons out, I test the seeds by putting 10 or 20 of them in a moist paper towel, then insert that into a plastic zipper bag. I put the bag on top of the fridge and check it every few days. If more than 50 percent germinate, I'll keep them; if not, it's into the compost bin.

Most seed savers are pleasantly surprised the next spring with germination rates. You'll be giving plants away before you know it.

When winter drags on, open one of those jars of basil seeds to get a good whiff of summer. It will make the season go a little quicker. Better yet, take those seeds out and start a few under lights, for the real thing.

Easy Spicy Basil Chicken

This recipe is one of my favorites and it's a good way to get rid of all those hot peppers at the end of the season. Now, it's got some fire, so if you're like me and love spicy food, give it a try. If not, reduce the hot chili peppers to a level you can tolerate. It's a great recipe no matter what.

What You Need:

2 tablespoons chili oil
2 tablespoons good olive oil
5 cloves fresh garlic, chopped
3 hot chili peppers, cut into small pieces
   (I like red cayenne peppers. Remove the
   seeds and inner fleshy walls to reduce the
   heat unless you really like to turn it up)
1 pound skinless, boneless
   chicken breast halves, cubed

1½ teaspoons white sugar
Sea salt and fresh ground pepper to taste
6 tablespoons oyster sauce
1½ cup fresh mushrooms, chopped
1 cup onions, minced
2 cups fresh basil leaves, chopped roughly,
   leaving some leaves whole

Here's How:

In a medium saucepan, cook the chili oil, olive oil and garlic, using the "exploding garlic" technique (see recipe for Simple Red Sauce on page 74). Add chili peppers and cook for about 2 or 3 minutes more.

Add the chicken and sugar, and season with salt and pepper. Cook until chicken is no longer pink, but not done – about 5 to 10 minutes.

Stir oyster sauce into the skillet. Mix onions and continue cooking until they start to soften, then add mushrooms. Continue cooking until chicken is done.

Remove from heat and mix in the basil. Let sit for a couple minutes to let the leaves wilt before serving.

Serves 2 to 4.

APPENDIX

Favorite Resources

For seeds:

W. Atlee Burpee & Co.
Warminster, PA
800-333-5808
www.burpee.com

Heirloom Seeds
724-663-5356
www.heirloomseeds.com
(They no longer print a catalog and
orders are online only)

Baker Creek Heirloom Seeds
Mansfield, MO
417-924-8917
www.rareseeds.com

Totally Tomatoes
Randolph, WI
800-345-5977
www.totallytomato.com

Tomato Growers Supply Company
Fort Myers, FL
888-478-7333
www.tomatogrowers.com

Good places to buy garlic:

Bobba-Mike's Gourmet Garlic Farm
Orrville, OH
www.garlicfarm.com
Bob and Wendy offer top quality
garlic at a great price.

Enon Valley Garlic
Enon Valley, PA
724-336-0501
www.EnonValleyGarlic.com

Peaceful Valley Farm Supply
Grass Valley, CA
888-784-1722
www.groworganic.com

For organic pest and disease controls – if you can't find any locally:

Gardens Alive
Lawrenceburg, IN
513-354-1482
www.gardensalive.com

Soil Tests: available at your local co-operative extension agency or these independent labs:

Woods End Soil Labs
Mt. Vernon, ME
207-293-2457
www.woodsend.org

A&L Agricultural Labs
Richmond. VA
804-743-9401
www.al-labs-west.com/agriculture.htm

Peaceful Valley Farm Supply
Grass Valley, CA
888-784-1722
www.groworganic.com

Organic Fertilizer:

Ohio Earth Food
Hartville, OH
330-877-9356
www.ohioearthfood.com
This company has the best quality fertilizer I've
ever seen. Re-Vita Compost Plus is a pelletized
formula I use religiously in the garden. Their
organic potting soil is awesome too.

ACKNOWLEDGMENTS

To Cindy, for standing beside me through everything and being my one true love forever. To my family, for letting me tell our stories of a life together and putting up with my work schedule.

To George Ball, Jr., President of W. Atlee Burpee & Co., for his generous foreword . . . and for his devoted work supporting the benefits and pleasures of home-grown food.

A thank-you to Chef Chris Jackson of Ted and Honey Café Market in Brooklyn, for permission to include his excellent recipes.

Thanks to Chef Donato Coluccio of Pittsburgh's Capital Grille, for sharing his recipes and teaching me about exploding garlic.

To Pittsburgh chef Brandy Stewart, for the delectable hazelnut pesto recipe.

To Chester Aaron, for being such a great writer, for loving garlic so much, and for kind permission to include three of his favorite recipes.

To Paul Kelly, my publisher, for coming up with the idea for this book and having faith in me that I could write it.

To Cathy Dees, my editor, for turning my words into prose; and to Abby Dees, for putting my recipes in good order.

Thanks to Dan and Lynnete Yarnick of Yarnick's Farms in Indiana, PA, for the beautiful produce on the cover. If you're out their way, they welcome visitors to their farm.

To Sirius XM's Little Steven's Underground Garage, for keeping me sane as my deadline loomed. I listened to it a lot while writing (along with my catalog of Stones bootlegs). The music inspired me to be creative like the cool artists I was listening to, occasionally picking up my Fender Telecaster to strum along. "The Man Who Shot Liberty Valance" kept me going one long summer day while I was stuck in front of the computer writing about garden tools and weeds.

ABOUT THE AUTHOR

Doug Oster is the *Pittsburgh Post-Gazette's* "Backyard Gardener." A regular guest on Martha Stewart's "Morning Living" Sirius XM radio show, Doug is the garden expert on "Pittsburgh Today Live" (KDKA-TV) and co-hosts the "The Organic Gardeners," the popular Sunday show on KDKA radio. He also writes a nationally syndicated herb and cooking column.

Doug is co-author of two books: *Grow Organic* and *A Gardener's Journal.* In 2009, he wrote, produced and hosted the one-hour PBS documentary, "The Gardens of Pennsylvania," for which he won an Emmy.

The author lives with his wife Cindy and three children on four well-composted acres near Pittsburgh.

Visit Doug on the web at:

www.dougoster.com

www.theorganicgardeners.com

INDEX

RECIPE FINDER

Also available:

GROW ORGANIC
OVER 250 TIPS AND IDEAS FOR GROWING
FLOWERS, VEGGIES, LAWNS AND MORE

By Doug Oster and Jessica Walliser

For gardening first-timers and old-timers alike, **Grow Organic** is an easy-access, step-by-step guide to growing organic. Doug Oster and Jessica Walliser have written this friendly, authoritative book for anyone who dreams of having a beautiful lawn, fruits and veggies to die for, a flower bed that just won't stop – and a garden environment where all of nature can thrive without pesticides.

Grow Organic can be purchased at book stores nationwide and online booksellers ($18.95, St. Lynn's Press).

www.theorganicgardeners.com

www.stlynnspress.com